Questioning
FOR Classroom Discussion

ASCD MEMBER BOOK

Many ASCD members received this book as a
member benefit upon its initial release.

Learn more at: **www.ascd.org/memberbooks**

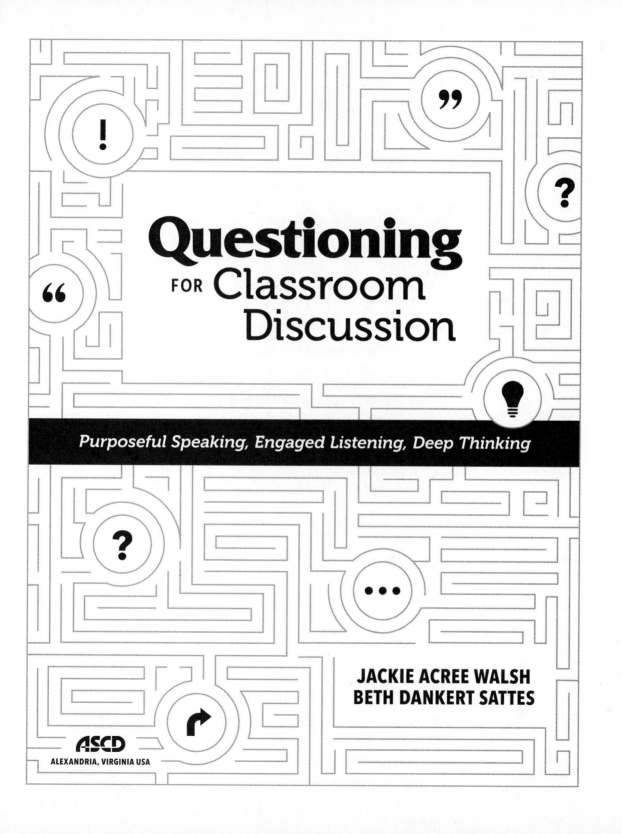

Questioning
FOR Classroom
Discussion

Purposeful Speaking, Engaged Listening, Deep Thinking

JACKIE ACREE WALSH
BETH DANKERT SATTES

ASCD
ALEXANDRIA, VIRGINIA USA

1703 N. Beauregard St. • Alexandria, VA 22311-1714 USA
Phone: 800-933-2723 or 703-578-9600 • Fax: 703-575-5400
Website: www.ascd.org • E-mail: member@ascd.org
Author guidelines: www.ascd.org/write

Deborah S. Delisle, *Executive Director;* Stefani Roth, *Publisher;* Genny Ostertag, *Director, Content Acquisitions;* Julie Houtz, *Director, Book Editing & Production;* Jamie Greene, *Editor;* Melissa Johnston, *Graphic Designer;* Mike Kalyan, *Manager, Production Services;* Kyle Steichen, *Senior Production Specialist;* Keith Demmons, *Production Designer*

PAPERBACK ISBN: 978-1-4166-2098-3   ASCD product #115012
PDF E-BOOK ISBN: 978-1-4166-2099-0; see Books in Print for other formats.

Quantity discounts: 10–49, 10%; 50+, 15%; 1,000+, special discounts (e-mail programteam@ascd.org or call 800-933-2723, ext. 5773, or 703-575-5773). For desk copies, go to www.ascd.org/deskcopy.

ASCD Member Book No. FY16-2 (Nov. 2015 PSI+). ASCD Member Books mail to Premium (P), Select (S), and Institutional Plus (I+) members on this schedule: Jan, PSI+; Feb, P; Apr, PSI+; May, P; Jul, PSI+; Aug, P; Sep, PSI+; Nov, PSI+; Dec, P. For current details on membership, see www.ascd.org/membership.

Library of Congress Cataloging-in-Publication Data

Walsh, Jackie A.
 Questioning for classroom discussion : purposeful speaking, engaged listening, deep thinking / by Jackie Acree Walsh & Beth Dankert Sattes.
     pages cm
 Includes bibliographical references and index.
 ISBN 978-1-4166-2098-3 (pbk. : alk. paper) 1. Questioning. 2. Discussion. I. Sattes, Beth D. (Beth Dankert) II. Title.
 LB1027.44.W36 2015
 371.3'7--dc23
                              2015029947

23 22 21 20 19 18 17 16 15   1 2 3 4 5 6 7 8 9 10 11 12

Questioning FOR Classroom Discussion

ACKNOWLEDGMENTS

Countless individuals provided the inspiration, encouragement, and support that enabled us to undertake and complete this project.

Allison Scott, ASCD Acquisitions Editor, encouraged us from the inception to the conclusion of this project. Allison identified the need for a book that would provide a practical approach to developing student skills for discussion. She posed thoughtful questions as we conceptualized the book's framework and provided helpful feedback in early drafts. Not only did she offer wise counsel related to the substance of the book, she was unswerving in her patience and understanding throughout the process.

Cristina Solis, a passionate and deeply committed practitioner, first invited us to design a professional learning experience for administrators focused on the connections between our work in quality questioning and "Questioning and Discussion," indicator 3b in the Danielson Framework for Effective Teaching. Through dialogue with Cristina, we developed new insights that led us to think about the possibility of writing a book such as this. In the midst of writing the book, Cristina provided the opportunity for us to validate the frameworks underpinning this book as we provided professional development to groups of NYC teachers, principals, and instructional coaches. We value Cristina as a thought partner, colleague, and friend.

We share a passion for working with teachers and school leaders in over-time professional learning that focuses on the reflection of questioning practices. Through the years, we have interacted with thousands of educators across the country, and we have learned from the experience and craft knowledge they have shared with us. We are particularly grateful to the teachers whose classrooms are featured throughout this book. Additionally, we acknowledge below the school leaders who enabled us to work with these teachers.

As we were embarking on this project, our work with Sharon Hill, former principal of PS 290, Manhattan New School, and her amazing faculty expanded our understanding of questioning for discussion in the elementary grades. Paige Meloni, executive director of student and academic services, SCUC (TX) ISD, has enabled us to connect with teachers and students in their classroom settings and thereby include a number of their voices in the text. Principal Lisa Berry and her faculty at Hewitt-Trussville Middle School (AL) opened their classrooms and provided videos that served as grist for certain sections of the book. Naomi Isaac-Simpson championed our work in NYC and NJ schools, taking it into classrooms and sharing countless examples of discussion in elementary schools, particularly in math classrooms. Cheryl Altizer, principal at Ansted Elementary in Fayette County (WV), and her staff welcomed us into their school to learn together about ways to engage K–5 students in discussion.

We are grateful to the Teaching Channel for their permission to connect to selected videos via the use of QR codes and to the individual teachers whose classrooms are featured in these videos.

All authors stand on the shoulders of thinkers and writers whose work they have read and reflected on over time. We feel particularly indebted to James T. Dillon, professor emeritus at UC Riverside, whose work on questioning and discussion influenced us early on in our work together. Dillon's distinction between questioning in recitation and questioning for discussion continues to drive our thinking.

Carla McClure carefully read our draft manuscript and provided helpful feedback. Carla has served as an important critical friend to us over many years. We value her intellect, wit, and friendship.

Jackie is grateful for the inspiration provided by her children, Catherine and Will, both of whom are extraordinary questioners and facilitators of discussion with university students. She also wishes to acknowledge the intellectual stimulation and moral support provided by a valued colleague, Cathy Gassenheimer, executive vice president for the Alabama Best Practices Center.

Beth is indebted to her mother for first teaching her the value of discussions—around the dining room table—on a variety of subjects, none ever too controversial. She continues to learn through discussions with her husband, Lyle, and her sons Chris and Michael—all of whom have supported her work, despite the days and hours it has taken her away from home.

Finally, we appreciate Jamie Greene's careful and thoughtful reading and review of the manuscript. As an associate editor with ASCD, he managed the editing and review process in an efficient manner and enhanced the quality of the final product.

INTRODUCTION

Making the Case for Questioning for Discussion

Why should we place greater emphasis on questioning for discussion in our classrooms?

Questioning and discussion are important means—and ends—of student learning. Research connects student engagement through questioning and discussion to improved learning outcomes, including higher levels of thinking and increases in student achievement (Applebee et al., 2003; Murphy et al., 2009). Furthermore, the skills of questioning and discussion are valuable in and of themselves. Employers report that they are important to career success (Wagner, 2008), college professors tout their value in the academic environment (Conley, 2008; Graff, 2003), and which of us would not agree that discussion and critical thinking skills are keys to active citizenship in our democratic society?

Questioning and discussion work in tandem to move students from passive participants to active meaning makers. Acknowledgment of the interdependent nature of these two skills can be found in the new state standards and in teacher evaluation rubrics. Advocates for an increased focus on questioning and discussion argue that these skills support critical thinking and collaborative problem solving (Schmoker, 2006; Wagner, 2010).

Given the compelling case for the value of questioning for discussion, one might assume that these instructional strategies are used effectively and regularly in K–12 classrooms throughout the United States. However, there is substantial research to the contrary: classroom discussion is a rare event in our schools. Perhaps this is one reason for the current emphasis on questioning and discussion in curriculum standards and teacher evaluation systems. Skillful use of questioning for discussion is clearly a classroom practice that is worthy of pursuit.

Questioning and Discussion: Prominent in Learning and Teaching Standards

A signal feature of the Common Core State Standards (CCSS) is the inclusion of *speaking and listening* alongside *reading* and *writing* in the triumvirate of English language arts (ELA)/literacy standards. The underlying logic is that these three skill sets are interdependent and reinforce one another in deepening students' understanding of content. This logic is evident in the first CCSS anchor standard for speaking and listening, which states that students should be able to do the following:

> Prepare for and participate effectively in a range of conversations and collaborations with diverse partners, building on others' ideas and expressing their own clearly and persuasively. (ELA-Literacy.CCRA.SL.1)

The conjunction of discussion and questioning appears in the grade-level Common Core standards associated with this anchor, beginning with kindergarten. By the time students are in Grades 11–12, they are expected to do the following:

> Propel conversations by posing and responding to questions that probe reasoning and evidence; ensure a hearing for a full range of positions on a topic or issue; clarify, verify, or challenge ideas and conclusions; and promote divergent and creative perspectives. (ELA-Literacy.SL11-12.1C)

Similar language appears in the speaking and listening standards of all non-CCSS states. For example, here's one of Virginia's English Standards of Learning (SOL) for Grades 9–10: "Move conversations ahead by posing and responding to questions, actively involve others in the discussion, and challenge ideas" (10.1 CF). Likewise, the state standards for Texas—the Texas Essential Knowledge and Skills (TEKS)—contain a strong speaking and listening strand that involves student questioning and collaborative conversations.

Thanks to the Common Core Standards for Mathematical Practice (http://www.corestandards.org/Math/Practice), many mathematics classrooms today are alive with student discussion. Even though questioning and thinking support all eight of these standards, it is Mathematical Practice Standard 3 that requires particular teacher and student skills in questioning for discussion: "Construct viable arguments and critique the reasoning of others" (CCSS.Math.Practice.MP3). More specifically, this standard requires that students "justify their conclusions, communicate them to others, and respond to the arguments of others" and that "students at all grades listen or read the arguments of others, decide whether they make sense, and ask useful questions to clarify or improve the arguments."

A look at the Next Generation Science Standards (NGSS) reveals that four of the eight NGSS science practices directly relate to questioning or discussion: asking questions; constructing explanations; engaging in argument from evidence; and obtaining, evaluating, and communicating information. Moreover, the inquiry-based nature of science lends itself to student dialogue as learners hypothesize and speculate, test and evaluate results, and work collaboratively to make sense of their experiments.

The College, Career, and Civic Life Framework (the "C3"), released in 2013 by the National Council for the Social Studies, features an "inquiry arc" with four dimensions that span the social science disciplines: developing questions and planning inquiries; applying disciplinary concepts and tools; evaluating sources and using evidence; and communicating conclusions and taking informed action. The emphasis on questioning and discussion is apparent.

Not surprisingly, speaking and listening, within the context of academic conversations or discussions, are central to the English Language Proficiency (ELP) standards developed by the Teachers of English to Speakers of Other Languages (TESOL). All five ELP standards focus on communication, and Standard 1 is "English language learners communicate for social, intercultural, and instructional purposes within the school setting" (TESOL, 2006, p. 28). Fisher and Frey (2008) emphasize oral language as the bridge between reading and writing: "Oral language tasks do not end with the conversation but serve to scaffold learning, allowing students to activate their thinking before they read or to clarify their understanding and their use of language in preparation to write" (p. 41).

Even as discussion is a focus for learning standards, so is it also an important component of research-based rubrics underpinning current teacher evaluation frameworks. For example, Charlotte Danielson's Framework for Teaching, one of the two most widely used evaluation systems in the United States (Popham, 2013, p. 61), spotlights questioning and discussion. Questioning and Discussion (3b) are the "only instructional strategies specifically referred to in the Framework for Teaching, a decision that reflects their central "importance to teachers' practice." Danielson views discussion and questioning as strategies for deepening understanding (personal communication, December 10, 2014).

Three elements associated with questioning and discussion form the related component in Danielson's framework. These elements are (1) quality of questions/prompts, (2) discussion techniques, and (3) student participation. Danielson's rubric includes four levels for rating teacher quality: Distinguished, Proficient, Basic, and Unsatisfactory. The Distinguished level for the questioning and discussion component requires proactivity on the part of students in asking questions, challenging one another's thinking, and making comments. Inherent in this expectation is the assumption that teachers are developing student skills in these areas and creating a classroom culture where students are comfortable exercising these responsibilities. This sophisticated view of teacher responsibility is one that we propose in this book.

> **Danielson Framework for Teaching**
> **Component 3b: Using Questioning and Discussion Techniques**
> **Distinguished (Level 4)**
>
> The teacher uses a variety or series of questions or prompts to challenge students cognitively, advance high-level thinking and discourse, and promote metacognition. Students formulate many questions, initiate topics, challenge one another's thinking, and make unsolicited contributions. Students themselves ensure that all voices are heard in the discussion. (Danielson, 2013, p. 67)

The current emphasis on questioning and discussion raises this question: What is the state of the art and practice of classroom questioning, particularly as it supports student discussion? If you assume that this emphasis is born of a perceived need or an identified gap between best practice and actual documented practice, then the following will affirm your thinking.

Discussion: A Rare Occurrence in K–12 Classrooms

Educational thought leaders have long lamented the limited opportunity for student interaction in K–12 classrooms. More than 30 years ago, Ernest Boyer, reporting on secondary education in the United States, wrote the following:

> Most discussion in classrooms, when it occurs, calls for simple recall (*What were the provisions of the Treaty of 1763?*) or the application of an idea (*Use the periodic table to find an atomic number*). Occasionally students are asked to develop explanations (*If we were to release ammonia in one corner of the room, why is it possible to smell it in the opposite corner?*). But serious intellectual discussion is rare. (Boyer, 1983, p. 146)

Likewise, John Goodlad (1984), lead researcher in the landmark Study of Schooling, reported that discussion—which he defined as interactions between a teacher and students—constituted, on average, only about 5 percent of class time. This study collected and analyzed data from more than 1,000 K–12 classroom observations.

Little has changed since then, as researchers continue to find that true discussion is rarely present in K–12 classrooms. For example, Kamil and colleagues (2008) report that "discussion currently accounts for an average of only 1.7 minutes per 60 minutes of classroom instruction, with classrooms varying between 0 and slightly more than 14" (p. 22). That's less than 3 percent of classroom time! Teachers who read this statistic might be tempted to say, "That's not true in *my* classroom," but the gap between what we *think* we do and what we *actually* do can be larger than we might think. Consider the following finding by Applebee (1996): "Although middle and high school teachers report that 'discussion' is their primary instructional format, in a study of 112 eighth- and ninth-grade language arts classes, researchers found that students engaged in less than one minute of true discussion per hour of class" (p. 87). Further, the Learning 24/7 Study of 1,500 classrooms found "evidence of academic dialog and discussion in only 0.5 percent" of classrooms observed (Schmoker, 2006, p. 66).

A number of large-scale studies of teaching practice have used the Danielson framework for a segment of their data collection. For example, the MET study, funded by the Gates Foundation, trained and certified observers to collect data using this framework. Of the 10 components that can be observed in the classroom, 3b (discussion) received the lowest ratings; that is, discussion was the area in which teachers had the most difficulty achieving an Above Basic rating (Ho & Kane, 2013).

Parallel results were found in another large study conducted by the Consortium on Chicago School Research at the University of Chicago Urban Education Institute. On Danielson's 3b component, 41–45 percent of teachers received an Unsatisfactory or Basic rating. Indeed, a much higher percentage of teachers received substantially lower ratings in this component than they did in the other nine observable components (Sartain et al., 2011). Clearly, these studies indicate that higher-level questioning and discussion are not present in most classrooms.

Tony Wagner (2010) adds another source to these quantitative data: student voice. In *The Global Achievement Gap*, he writes, "My interviews with students, as well as with their high school and college teachers, confirm that students are increasingly impatient with the lecture style of teaching and the reliance on textbooks for information, and crave more discussion" (p. 178).

Questioning for Discussion

For more than two decades, we've worked intensively with classroom teachers to enhance their use of classroom questioning. From the beginning, we've made a distinction between questioning for discussion and questioning in recitation. Recitation, the dominant form of classroom discourse, follows a pattern known as IRE (Initiate, Response, Evaluate). In other words, the teacher asks a question for which there is a "right" answer, calls on one student to answer, and evaluates that student's response. Although this pattern of questioning serves some essential instructional purposes—particularly during the early stages of the learning cycle—IRE does not encourage an "exploration of ideas, which is essential to the development of understanding of discussion-based approaches in teaching for understanding" (Applebee, 2003, p. 685).

Questions that promote deep engagement in the analysis, evaluation, and synthesis of ideas are of a completely different order than those used in recitation to determine if students are learning facts or building the expected knowledge base. Questions for discussion are divergent, not convergent; that is, they are open to different interpretations and conclusions, not closed to one "right" answer. They engage students in higher-level processing of information, moving beyond the mere regurgitation of textbook or teacher answers. They spark internal debates within a student's mind, either through the creation of cognitive dissonance or the presentation of an authentic challenge or issue.

Questions that promote deep engagement . . . spark internal debates within a student's mind.

Many questioning strategies that are useful for igniting and sustaining the type of thinking required for a true discussion differ significantly from those used in recitation. True discussions cannot occur through use of the IRE model, in which the teacher is the pivot point and filter for all student talk. Rather, the point of true discussion is for students to exchange ideas with one another and engage in a conversation with their peers. While the teacher does not abdicate responsibility for monitoring the appropriateness and quality of student talk, the goal is to sustain student thinking and student-to-student interactions. In particular, the teacher resists the temptation to evaluate every student comment, either positively or negatively. Rather than offer questions at every turn of talk, as in recitation, the teacher encourages students to question, agree, or disagree with one another, and provide rationales for their positions. When the teacher enters the discussion, it is often to participate in the flow of ideas.

Moving classroom conversations from recitations to discussions doesn't happen on its own. It requires commitment, intentionality, and practice. Most of us have had limited opportunity to learn about and participate in true discussions, either as students or in our professional training. This is also true for our students, who have the additional handicap of living in a culture dominated by 24-hour news channels whose political panels tend toward "uncivil discord" rather than "civil discourse."

This book is for teachers who wish to change student outcomes by changing the conversation—their own and that of their students. It offers a framework, strategies, and tools for planning and facilitating classroom discussions that help students develop the skills and dispositions needed for college, career, citizenship, and a meaningful and productive life. It is also for school leaders who are seeking a deeper personal understanding of what exemplary classroom discussion looks and sounds like and who are committed to working with teachers across their schools to improve this powerful approach to learning.

Organization of This Book

The kind of discussion described in this book requires both teachers and students not only to master new skills and adopt new dispositions but also to unlearn habits and behaviors that have long been associated with the way we "do school." The book is organized to help readers understand why and how we can cultivate classrooms for productive discussion.

Chapter 1 explains how four practices of quality questioning support thoughtful discussion: (1) framing of focus questions to initiate and sustain student thinking and interactions, (2) promoting the equitable participation of all students to ensure they are responsible for formulating responses and contributing to the discussion, (3) scaffolding of student comments to sustain and deepen thinking and understanding, and (4) creating a classroom culture that supports thoughtful and respectful discourse.

Chapter 2 presents four capacities associated with productive discussion that teachers can develop in their students: social skills, cognitive skills, use-of-knowledge skills, and supportive dispositions. By explicitly teaching students how each of these contributes to productive discussion, and by providing opportunities for students to practice and refine these skills and dispositions, teachers can help students develop the facility to engage in disciplined discussion.

We identify three distinct forms of discussion (see Figure A) that constitute practice fields for student discussion: teacher-guided discussion, structured small-group discussion, and student-driven discussion. These three forms exist on a continuum from "more teacher control" to "more student responsibility," and each has inherent value at different stages in the learning cycle. Through the purposeful use of teacher-guided and structured small-group discussions, teachers can scaffold students' development of skills and dispositions needed for effective discussions—and prepare students to engage in successful student-driven discussions at appropriate moments in the learning cycle.

Figure A | **Three Forms of Discussion**

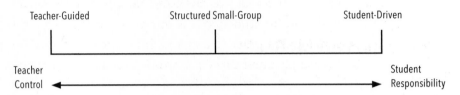

Chapter 3 focuses on teacher-guided discussions, in which the teacher assumes an active role in facilitating student talk. Teachers do this by being intentional as they offer comments, pose questions, and make other explicit moves to shape students' cognitive engagement in a classroom conversation and deepen student understanding of content. Teachers model, scaffold, and coach as they help students develop skills and dispositions associated with productive discussion. Teacher-guided discussion can occur in whole-class or small-group settings. The chapter presents a five-stage process for planning, implementing, and reflecting on discussion. This structure can help teachers be more thoughtful and intentional in planning for and guiding productive discussions.

Chapter 4 addresses structured small-group discussion, which occurs when teachers strategically assign students to small groups and use guidelines and protocols to structure conversation. For instance, the teacher might delineate student roles and responsibilities, provide step-by-step directions or questions for exploring a topic, or use text-based protocols. The structures embedded in small groups scaffold the development of three categories of social skills associated with discussion—speaking, listening, and collaborating—and advance cognitive and use-of-knowledge skills. They also nurture related dispositions.

Chapter 5 explores student-driven discussion. In this type of discourse, students assume primary responsibility for leading the discussion, adhere to selected guidelines, and often operate within a framework such as Paideia or Socratic seminars. The keys to successful student-driven discussion are ensuring that students understand their roles and responsibilities in this environment, selecting an appropriate text or topic for discussion, and minimizing teacher intervention into the conversation. It is in this arena that students are free to explore topics with minimal teacher intervention as they integrate knowledge from different spheres and create new ways of thinking about issues.

Chapter 6 provides readers with a retrospective on the frameworks, tools, and resources provided throughout this book and an opportunity to reflect on how to use these with and for students. It is our hope that you will find this book to be a useful manual of practice and a hands-on resource that you will turn to frequently as you plan and carry out productive classroom discussions with your students.

Committing to the Journey

We conceive of this book as a resource for K–12 teachers across all disciplines and for instructional leaders who coach and support them. To this end, we have included a range of tools and resources from which you can select the skills and strategies most appropriate to the particular grade level(s) and content area(s) you teach. We suggest that readers begin with Chapters 1 and 2 prior to moving to other chapters. These chapters provide the foundation on which Chapters 3–5 rest. Although the forms of discussion presented in Chapters 3, 4, and 5 can build on one another, these chapters can stand alone and be read in any order.

Questioning and discussion have high potential for engaging students at the highest levels of thinking and learning. The extent to which this potential is realized, of course, depends on individual teachers who embrace these practices and make them their own, use them as vehicles for connecting disciplinary knowledge to the hearts and minds of their students, and realize that this pathway involves a true partnership with their students. We hope that this book will inspire you to recommit to this journey and help you take your students to greater heights.

Reflecting and Connecting

Reflect on where you and your students are in the use of questioning for discussion in your classroom and school. What is your vision for questioning for discussion with your students? What do you hope to gain from reading and reflecting on this book?

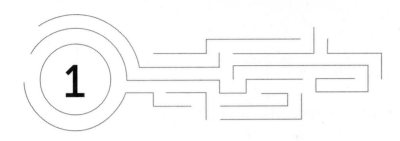

Quality Questioning: The Heart of Thoughtful Discussion

What type of questioning invigorates and sustains productive discussions?

Quality questioning is at the heart of skillful and thoughtful student discussion. Teachers who learn to ask quality questions, and teach their students to do the same, can transform typical classroom interactions by involving students in purposeful speaking, engaged listening, and deep thinking. Cognitive demand increases as students are expected to formulate their own questions—rather than wait for the teacher's—as they speak and listen to their peers, not just to the teacher. The practice of quality questioning empowers students to engage in challenging forms of discourse that require openness, respect for different points of view, and persistence to develop new understandings.

A well-conceived, stimulating question is a catalyst for the type of student thinking that leads to such purposeful speaking and listening. Follow-up comments or questions elicit evidence and surface reasoning to ensure rigor in thinking. Respect for "think time" enables students to go deeper in their own thinking and that of their classmates. Practices that support the thinking of all and scaffold students' participation ensure the expression of diverse points of view. Purposeful responses to students' comments can sustain their thinking.

A teacher's use of these questioning practices provides a structure that supports student thinking through discussion—and offers a model for students to follow as they assume increasing responsibility for managing discourses with their peers. When these practices occur within a culture that celebrates thinking, thoughtful and productive discussion results.

Distinguishing Between Questioning for Discussion and in Recitation

J. T. Dillon's *Questioning and Teaching: A Manual of Practice* (1988) has contributed greatly to our thinking about classroom questioning. Dillon draws a distinction between questioning practices that promote recitation, the usual form of classroom talk, and those that foster discussion, a type of interaction that rarely occurs in K–12 classrooms. Since the publication of his book in 1988, little has changed in U.S. classrooms: recitation, or what many researchers dub IRE (Initiate, Response, Evaluate) (Mehan, 1979), continues to be the dominant form of classroom talk. Gordon Wells (1993) refers to this back-and-forth talk between the teacher and one student at a time as IRF (Initiation, Response, Feedback). Given the current emphasis on formative assessment and feedback, IRF is perhaps a more accurate depiction of what happens in a productive classroom recitation.

Dillon's observations about the differences between questioning in recitation and questioning for discussion seem as relevant today as ever. Dillon distinguishes between the purposes of questioning in these two contexts and the characteristics of the questions themselves. Over the years, teachers with whom we work have affirmed the utility of this distinction, and we have deepened our understanding of these differences through our own explorations. Figure 1.1 presents several distinctions between the purposes of questioning in recitation and for discussion. As you review this information, you will likely infer that recitation is the setting in which teachers structure student mastery of core knowledge and fundamental skills, whereas discussion is the arena in which students think critically or creatively about that knowledge and have opportunities to integrate it more deeply into their mental frames.

Figure 1.1 | **A Comparison of the Purposes of Questioning in Recitation and for Discussion**

Purposes of Questioning	
In Recitation	**For Discussion**
• To develop foundational knowledge and skills • To provide drill and practice opportunities • To check for understanding by generating formative feedback for teacher and student • To build individual accountability* • To encourage student self-assessment* • To cue students on what's important to know • To encourage student (not teacher) talk*	• To personalize meaning and connect to prior understandings • To extend or deepen thinking • To deepen understanding of concepts by questioning and making new connections • To listen in order to understand and appreciate diverse points of view • To learn how to disagree in a civil manner • To reflect on one's own and others' beliefs • To develop a life skill important for working in groups

* These characteristics apply to discussion and recitation.

Let us be clear: questioning in recitation is no less important to teaching and learning than questioning for discussion. The point that Dillon makes, and one with which we concur, is that they have very different purposes. Questioning in recitation serves the critically important purpose of checking for understanding. In this context, teachers pose questions for the purpose of formative assessment. Dylan Wiliam (2011) refers to these questions as "hinge-point questions" and suggests they should be part of an instructional sequence. The purpose of such questions is to determine if students are ready to move forward or if they require reteaching. Not only does questioning in recitation provide teachers with formative feedback, but, when properly managed, it also engages students in reflecting on the extent to which they know or understand facts and concepts. Student self-assessment is the most powerful type of formative assessment.

Whereas questioning in recitation checks for understanding, questioning for discussion helps to build and deepen understanding and oftentimes occurs after students have mastered core content. As teachers plan lessons, they need to establish a clear purpose for any discussion included in their unit design—and thus about the purposes of questioning in those particular lessons.

Whatever the purpose of a specific discussion, however, a hallmark of teacher questioning for discussion is its intentionality in supporting students as they develop the skills and dispositions required for productive discussion.

Central to classroom questioning are the questions teachers frame to initiate and drive the process, whether the purpose is recitation or discussion. The characteristics of the questions teachers pose are key determinants of whether students engage in a recitation or discussion:

> Although discussion resembles recitation in that students and teachers are talking back and forth, discussion is a process with characteristics of its own, entailing a characteristic use of questions to facilitate the process. Therefore, the use of questions appropriate to recitation promises only to foil discussion, turning it into something like a recitation. (Dillon, 1988, p. 119)

Figure 1.2, which draws heavily from Dillon's thinking, shows the contrasting characteristics of questions in these two contexts. Most teachers, when asked, say questions for discussion are open-ended and invite student thinking, whereas questions in recitation seek to determine if students know key facts and concepts. However, not all teachers recognize that one well-thought-out question for discussion can propel a discussion for an entire class period.

Questioning to Promote Thoughtful Discussion

A thoughtful and productive classroom discussion is like a colorful, tightly woven tapestry, as its many threads intertwine in purposeful ways and result in discernable patterns. Like a fine tapestry, a productive discussion does not just happen; it results from planning and skilled craftsmanship. In the case of discussion, it is a teacher's and students' skills in quality questioning that underpin the successful outcome.

Ultimately, effective discussions depend on the knowledge and skills of those involved, which in classrooms are the students. However, most students do not come to school with the skills required for questioning and discussion. Therefore, teachers must plan for and model the use of questioning that leads to a productive discussion.

Figure 1.2 | **A Comparison of Questions Used in Recitation and for Discussion**

Characteristics of Questions	
In Recitation	**For Discussion**
• What is in question is whether the students know the teacher's (or the "correct") answer. • The teacher poses questions for which there are "right answers," which students have had the opportunity to learn. • Questions prompt students to recall or remember and/or to demonstrate understanding. • Questions are aligned with standards and learning targets.* • The teacher usually poses many questions.	• Questions are "true" or authentic questions. • Questions are open-ended and divergent—not convergent. • Questions stimulate responses at higher cognitive levels (Apply, Analyze, Evaluate, Create). • Questions engage students personally and emotionally. • The teacher poses one question for discussion; other questions emerge from both the students and the teacher.

* This applies to both recitation and discussion.

Entire books could be written about the art and science of asking quality questions. In fact, we've written a few ourselves! In those books, we define quality questioning as a process that includes preparation of questions as a part of lesson planning, presentation of questions in a manner that engages all students, prompting of student responses through the use of cues and probes, processing of student responses by providing feedback, and reflection on questioning practices (Walsh & Sattes, 2005, 2011).

In this book, however, we focus on ways teachers can draw from the following four practices associated with quality questioning as they plan for the meaningful engagement of their students in discussion:

- Framing focus questions that initiate and sustain student thinking and interactions.
- Promoting the equitable participation of everyone involved in the discussion.
- Scaffolding student responses to sustain and deepen thinking and understanding.
- Creating a culture that supports thoughtful and respectful discourse.

Each of these practices can be used for different purposes in different forms of discussion (e.g., teacher-guided, structured small-group, and student-driven). Like the beams on a loom, they form a structure on which students can weave a tapestry of ideas—in other words, a thoughtful discussion. When teachers consistently and intentionally put these beams into place as they plan and facilitate discussions, they also model for students how to build a discussion.

Questioning Practice #1: Frame a Quality Focus Question

Quality questions are catalysts for the generation and exchange of ideas that thread a productive discussion. Such questions do not typically emerge without effort; rather, they are the products of teachers thinking in a focused, exacting manner about the content under study. An important part of this effort is to identify and unpack the central ideas of standards and related content in search of an issue that will stimulate curiosity, controversy, or creativity.

Identify an issue. Framing a question that is powerful enough to drive a thoughtful discussion requires three steps. The first step is to identify an issue that will form the nucleus of the focus question. In the search for a viable candidate, teachers can test how well an issue might engage student thinking by considering the extent to which students (1) possess the depth and breadth of knowledge needed to wrestle with the issue, and (2) will be vested in the issue due to its relevance, importance, or intrinsic interest. McCann (2014), addressing discussion in the English language arts classroom, observes, "the point of entry into inquiry is the raising of doubt about subjects and issues that the learners care about." McCann points to topics that adolescents, in particular, will "energetically tackle"—equality, justice, responsibility, freedom, compassion, and loyalty: topics "that Shakespeare and thousands of other writers have grappled with for generations" (p. 25). The issue around which the question is framed must hold to a "shared point of doubt" for the students who will engage in the discussion (Haroutunian-Gordon, 2014). All of this is to say that the central issue embedded in a question must be sufficiently relevant and provocative to engage students emotionally.

> ### How to Frame a Quality Focus Question
> - Identify an issue.
> - Craft the question.
> - Anticipate student responses.

Craft the question. The second step in framing a quality focus question is to craft the question, which requires decisions about wording and syntax. Strong focus questions share a number of important characteristics:

- Academic vocabulary that is appropriate to the age and grade level of the students.
- Strong verbs intentionally chosen to activate student thinking at a particular level.
- A simple and straightforward sentence structure.
- Delivery within a meaningful context (teachers might need to prepare a statement that provides focus or context before asking the question).

The following vignette describes how a team used these principles in their collaborative work to frame a question.

The Case of a Revised Question

Members of an 8th grade social studies team collaboratively drafted the following question for use in a discussion at the culmination of a unit on ancient Athens: *Based on your knowledge of Athenian democracy, would implementing a direct democracy in our local government improve the quality of life?* This question focused on the content standard and related to the students' community. Good start. Of course, most readers will immediately notice that this is a yes-or-no question and add the follow-up "Why?" or "Provide reasons for your response."

On second look, however, team members began to question the potential of their question to engage students emotionally or cognitively. They decided that even though the question asked students to relate ancient history to the 21st century, they were unlikely to connect to it personally or to vest much emotional energy in the proposed discussion. Further, they determined that the cognitive demand of the question was relatively weak; it was lacking in academic vocabulary, including a strong thinking verb. After considerable reflection, the team modified the question. They decided to give the question to students several days in advance of the discussion to provide time for research and thinking. They also informed students that they would end the discussion with a vote to determine what the majority of students thought after exploring the issue together. This is their revision:

Imagine that our state legislature offered our local municipality the opportunity to operate as a direct democracy similar to that of ancient Athens.

- *Speculate as to the relative benefits and disadvantages of such a political structure for your and your family's quality of life—and for that of the community at large.*
- *Suggest how you might modify the system to make it more just.*
- *Support your ideas with cause-and-effect reasoning, specific examples, historical evidence, and other relevant information.*

Team members believe that their revised question has much greater potential for engaging students in a vibrant and productive discussion than did the original. The teachers hope students will be more vested in thinking about the question, given its stipulation that they consider personal and community impacts. Further, the teachers believe that having time in advance to gather information and think critically will enable students to collect evidence for their points of view. Perhaps, most important, the team feels that their revised question represents a more demanding cognitive task that requires students to speculate and support those speculations with evidence and reasoning. In fact, they conclude that this question will afford students practice in the type of thinking associated with good citizenship in our "democratic" society.

Anticipate student responses. The third step in framing a quality question is to anticipate alternative pathways that student thinking and interacting may take. During this step, teachers ask themselves, "How might my students respond to this question?" Teachers brainstorm and record possible student responses, taking into account both logical and defensible lines of reasoning and erroneous thinking. This exercise serves two purposes. First, it's a good check of whether the question, as written, has the capacity to produce a range of perspectives. This capacity is prerequisite to a rich and robust discussion in which students challenge one another's positions while staying open to rethinking their own. If a question cannot unlock multiple perspectives, then it is unlikely to lead to a thoughtful discussion. Teachers will want to reconsider the question if it does not tap into different points of view.

The second purpose for anticipating possible student responses is to plan effective teacher moves, either to sustain student thinking or, in the case of erroneous reasoning, to lead students to rethink or modify their positions. The ultimate goal is to develop students' skills in challenging, extending, and even correcting one another, but teachers need to be prepared to scaffold these processes, particularly when their students are relatively inexperienced or unskilled in discussion.

Predicting possible student responses to questions is the first practice recommended in The Five Practices Framework for promoting discussion in mathematics (Smith & Stein, 2011). Within that framework, "anticipating likely student responses to challenging mathematical tasks" requires teachers to generate multiple ways, both correct and incorrect, through which students might address challenging math problems (p. 8). Smith and Stein say this should be done as part of the planning process. They also suggest that when teachers create possible follow-up questions for each projected student response, they are better able to provide effective scaffolding and other follow-up moves during fast-paced classroom conversations. Such preparation equips teachers to help students correct their misunderstandings and extend their thinking. When teachers collaborate to generate likely responses and think together about alternative follow-up moves, they learn from and build upon one another's experiences, and the process is even more successful.

> Developing questions only "in the moment" is very challenging for a teacher who is juggling the needs of a classroom full of learners who need different types and levels of assistance. When teachers feel overwhelmed by the needs and frustrations of their students, it is easy for them to just revert to telling the students what to do when an alternative course of action does not imme-diately come to mind. (Smith & Stein, 2011, p. 36)

The Five Practices Framework has also been applied to science (Cartier et al., 2013). Anticipating how students are likely to respond to a task or question in science is particularly important, given that many students enter science class-rooms with deeply embedded misconceptions.

Let's return to "The Case of a Revised Question" and anticipate whether the final question will evoke a sufficient diversity of responses to make for a robust discussion. The revised question requires that students first understand the limitations of Athenian democracy. Students who possess this understand-ing may take conflicting positions related to the core issue. Some may focus on the disadvantages, pointing out that this culture rested on the backs of slaves. They may also take issue with the amount of time required for participation by large numbers of citizens and the resulting inefficiencies. Other students may concentrate on the benefits and propose structural changes to address what they deem to be the disadvantages. Those who lack foundational knowledge will have opportunities to correct their misunderstandings, as the question requires connection to the knowledge base. Anticipating possible directions the discussion may take, these teachers were able to talk about alternative moves they could make in response to identified student positions.

Questioning Practice #2: Promote Equitable Participation

A successful discussion is one that engages all students in thinking and exchanging ideas. Ensuring such a discussion is one of the greatest challenges teachers face as they prepare students for discussion and facilitate their engagement. To address this challenge, teachers need strategies for dealing with a number of difficult issues. For example: *How do we prevent eager and enthusiastic students from monopolizing talk without shutting them down? How do we encourage shy and reticent students without embarrassing them? How can we approach these issues without interfering with the rhythm of a discussion?* There are no simple answers. However, we suggest that teachers explore two strategies: (1) establish norms and guidelines that foster equitable participation, and (2) use structures that scaffold participation by all.

Because discussion is a significant deviation from ordinary classroom talk, it is important to be explicit about expectations for student engagement. The most important expectation to communicate is the belief that each student should be prepared to contribute. Carefully crafted participation norms build a culture in which students accept responsibility for their own and others' engagement in classroom discourse. We offer sample norms later in this chapter in our discussion of a classroom culture that supports questioning for discussion. The goal is for students both to "own" the participation norms associated with a culture for thoughtful discussion and to monitor and manage equitable participation independent of the teacher. However, because this is counter to traditional classroom behavior, teachers must lead students in developing and honoring norms that undergird equity. A first step in accomplishing this is to work with students to develop these guidelines. Once developed, teachers must keep the norms in front of students by posting and actively reviewing them before each classroom discussion.

One norm that is particularly counterintuitive to both students and teachers is that of no hand raising. In most schools, students learn from an early age to raise their hands to receive permission to speak. And, in most schools, teachers rely on volunteers—those with raised hands—to answer their questions. This practice leads to a large number of students opting out of classroom talk. We believe that allowing students to decide whether they want to participate has the effect of increasing the achievement gap. Like Dylan Wiliam (2011), we advocate that teachers decide who will respond to questions in recitation by using random methods for selecting respondents, engaging all students through alternative response strategies (e.g., signals, pair-talk, collaborative group work), or matching students with questions. In discussion, however, the no hand-raising policy is more about maintaining the flow of discussion by encouraging students to contribute as they are moved to speak. It is also about removing the teacher as the authority who decides who will speak when. The no hand-raising policy during discussions can open the door to a few more aggressive students monopolizing talk while the more reticent, less-assertive students have less (or no) talk time. It is for this reason that we suggest teachers use structures and norms to promote equitable participation.

Structures that scaffold participation by all can help normalize expected behaviors and assist students in becoming increasingly responsible for their own and their classmates' participation. In our work with teachers across the country, we have encountered countless strategies for building this type of student responsibility. Here are some of the most commonly used structures for scaffolding equitable participation.

Student trackers. Designate a few students to "keep track" of who has and has not spoken and to encourage classmates who have not spoken with prompts such as "What are you thinking about this?"

Fishbowl. Use a fishbowl protocol, wherein a limited number of students (five to seven) sit in an inner circle while other students sit in a concentric outer circle. Each student in the fishbowl is expected to contribute to the discussion, and the more forthcoming students seek to engage the more reticent ones by turning to them and asking for their thoughts. Those in the outer circle are expected to listen actively and take notes. The expectation should also be clear that they might need to go inside the fishbowl at some point to continue the conversation. The teacher may also ask those in the outer circle to keep track of how much everyone talks and to provide formative feedback when prompted. At the end of the fishbowl conversation, the teacher may ask students outside the fishbowl to share, in round-robin fashion, one thought related to what they heard. Some teachers then ask another group to move to the inner circle and continue the discussion or respond to another related prompt. Socratic seminars (discussed in Chapter 5) frequently use this format.

Short-answer round-robin. Ask each student to respond to a preliminary question in one or two words. For example, each student might be asked to select one adjective that best describes his or her personal reaction to a given topic. In round-robin fashion, each student offers a response and has the option of agreeing with a classmate. This strategy can level the playing field.

Small-group protocols. Use of small-group protocols assists in developing student accountability for personal participation and can also help students become sensitive to the need to encourage others to contribute their ideas. (See Chapter 4.)

Limitations on participation. Provide students with a limited number of tokens to "spend" during a discussion. Each time a student speaks, he or she relinquishes a token. When the tokens are gone, the student is no longer eligible to contribute orally to the conversation. This is our least favorite strategy, in part because it interferes with the natural flow of a discussion. Consider using it in the early stages of developing the norm of equity to heighten student awareness, and use it judiciously, especially with older students.

When teachers employ such structures, they need to be explicit with students about their reasons for doing so. Engage students in reflecting on their own and their peers' participation. Ask students to think about why it is valuable to hear from everyone. Set forth the expectation that class members take responsibility for supporting one another's engagement. As equitable participation becomes normalized, you can drop these scaffolds while continuing to encourage students to reflect on their individual involvement and on the extent to which the group encourages and supports everyone's voice being heard.

Questioning Practice #3:
Scaffold Student Responses to Deepen Thinking

Earlier we suggested that an important step in framing questions for discussion is the generation of possible teacher moves following anticipated student responses or comments. Such teacher moves, in the form of comments or questions, can scaffold student thinking. They can also shut it down. It all depends on the teacher's purpose, timing, and wording.

After years of classroom research, Dillon (1988) concluded that teacher interventions during student discussions tend to shut down student thinking and student talk. He found this to be particularly true of positive feedback or praise. The rationale, of course, is that when a teacher communicates agreement with one student's thinking, both the speaker and other classmates conclude that there is no need for further thought because the teacher has gotten the answer he or she was after.

Our view is that the type and frequency of teacher scaffolding varies in different forms of discussion. In teacher-guided discussion (see Chapter 3), the teacher is prepared to provide large doses of scaffolding to help students develop the social and cognitive skills required for disciplined discussion. Teacher-guided discussion is most appropriate when students are first learning the norms and processes of effective discussion or when the outcomes of the discussion are narrowly defined. Teachers enter such discussions with a full arsenal of follow-up questions and planned structures to corral student talk within established parameters. Likewise, in structured small-group discussions (see Chapter 4), teachers select specific protocols that support peer scaffolding of one another's thinking and engagement. Examples of scaffolding in both of these forms of discussion are included in later chapters.

Questioning Practice #4: Create a Culture for Thoughtful Discussion

Productive discussion is a collaborative endeavor that cannot take root in a competitive classroom where students believe they are vying against one another for teacher favor and high grades. Neither can thoughtful discussion thrive in a teacher-centered classroom with a right-answer orientation. Rather, it flourishes in a classroom community that celebrates curiosity, inquiry, and discovery. (In Chapter 2, you will learn more about teacher beliefs and student skills and dispositions that contribute to such a culture.)

While different forms of discussion call for varying guidelines or ground rules, a number of expectations or norms are common to all discussions. Three categories of norms support quality questioning: norms related to the purposes of questions, think times, and participation (Walsh & Sattes, 2011). These three categories of norms also support questioning for discussion. Though teachers often involve their students in creating their own class norms, the exemplars that follow can spur the readers' thinking about possibilities.

Three Categories of Norms in Questioning for Discussions

- Purposes of questions
- Think times
- Participation

Norms related to purposes of questions. When discussions proceed in a fluid and seamless manner, teachers and students understand that one well-crafted question establishes the boundaries for a productive discussion. Implicit in this understanding are three explicit shared understandings:

- **Use the focus question to stimulate and unlock your own thinking about the embedded issue or concept.** Students must believe that their teacher does not have a preconceived "best answer" or preferred position. Teachers take care not to impose their views or perspectives on their students.
- **Use the focus question to assist in zeroing in on what you know and think about the issue or concept embedded in the question.** An open-ended question does not mean that anything goes. Responsible discussants offer logic and evidence to support their positions; they draw upon their knowledge and experience related to the question. Those involved in the discussions, including the students and the teacher, hold one another accountable for engaging in responsible discussion. Remember our suggestion that teachers think in advance about criteria for acceptable responses?
- **Ask questions when you are curious, perplexed, or confused or when you need clarification.** Students understand that discussion is about wondering; asking questions; and digging deeper into issues, concepts, and differing perspectives. Teachers encourage students to surface their own questions as they engage with the content and with one another.

Norms related to think times. The honoring of silence is critical to a deep and productive discussion. Students recognize the benefits of silence as they clarify their own thinking and seek to understand the thinking of others. Silence in discussions builds on what we know about the value of Wait Time 1 and Wait Time 2. These two pauses, identified by Mary Budd Rowe (1986), support student thinking during all questioning contexts. Wait Time 1 is the pause after the asking of a question, before anyone responds. Wait Time 2 is the pause after someone speaks, before another speaker reacts. According to Rowe, the optimal time for each of these pauses is three to five seconds. While pausing at these two junctures is appropriate within a discussion, the three- to five-second length may not always be adequate. We believe three to five seconds should be considered as the floor, not the ceiling, for the length of pauses within discussion.

It is critical that students understand the purpose of the pauses or silence: to think. For this reason, we prefer to call these two pauses "think times" rather than wait times. The following three norms provide students with an explicit understanding of how to use these pauses.

- **Use think time to reflect.** When someone poses a question to you or comments on something you have said, take time to reflect on the question or comment and to think about your response to it.
- **Give others time to reflect.** Provide time to others who are thinking about their response to a question or comment.
- **Treat silence like gold.** Use silences during a discussion to process what others have said, rethink your own position, or consolidate thinking.

To make think time part of a classroom culture, students need to learn to become comfortable with and even celebrate silence. They live in a wider culture in which silence has become awkward and uncomfortable. Through discussion, students can learn that silence is a valuable resource—and a way of being together as people respect the thinking that can occur within the space created by silence.

Participation norms. A hallmark of effective classroom discussions is the extent to which all voices are heard over the course of time. To what extent are all students comfortable speaking? In what ways do students encourage their peers, particularly those who are quiet or reticent, to participate? Engaging all students is one of the greatest challenges for a teacher committed to creating a culture for effective classroom discussion. In later chapters, we suggest ways teachers can scaffold equitable participation during different forms of discussion. The following norms are appropriate in all settings:

- **Speak as you are motivated to speak, without raising your hand.** Hand raising is a difficult student habit to break; however, students need to learn how to interact in classroom conversations as they would in out-of-school conversations. Hand raising interrupts the flow of collaborative thinking.
- **Talk to one another, not to the teacher.** Students are conditioned to look to the teacher for affirmation; however, the purpose of discussions is for students to build on one another's ideas. Moving student desks into a configuration that allows them to look at one another when interacting can support this change.
- **Share what you are thinking so others can learn from you.** This norm is to encourage shy or reticent students, to convey to them that their thoughts are important and potentially valuable to other students.
- **Monitor your talk so as not to monopolize the conversation.** This is to remind talkative students that they should allow others the opportunity to participate.
- **Listen to others respectfully, asking questions to understand.** This norm undergirds a classroom culture where divergent thinking thrives, and students develop respect for those who hold different points of view. It also emphasizes the importance of questions to effective discussions.
- **Encourage others to speak, particularly those who are not participating.** In a vibrant discussion, students accept responsibility for participation by all by inviting peers who have not spoken to do so.

Students do not automatically understand the reasons for these norms, nor do they adopt them with ease. A number of these are counter to the school rules that students have learned and practiced over time. Young people must have opportunities to learn the reasons behind the norms and engage in intentional practice, followed by reflection and feedback.

The norms suggested above are neither exhaustive nor necessarily the right ones for your students. There is real value in engaging students in the development of norms for their own classroom conversations. The important thing is that we as teachers realize the need to make norms explicit.

Teachers cannot wave a wand or issue a mandate to create a culture that supports discussion. They can, however, lead the way as they model for students expected beliefs and behaviors and explicitly name and talk about critical components such as respect for others and their ideas, a willingness to take risks and learn from errors, the honoring of silence for thinking, tolerance for ambiguity, the inherent value of student questions, and other dispositions that support fruitful discussion. Teachers know they can't singlehandedly create the desired culture; they need to involve their students as co-creators of classroom communities. Giving students voice, ownership, and responsibility for their learning is critical to the emergence of the desired culture, and it is the essence of meaningful discussion.

Quality Questioning: A Handmaiden for Thoughtful Discussion

Many teachers think quality questioning means asking multiple questions and providing feedback. Their primary use of questioning is to control the substance of classroom talk—and students' participation in it. The practices associated with this approach to questioning, however, are not appropriate for true discussion.

Skillful teacher questioning supports true discussion when it initiates and sustains the conversation and when it nurtures and develops students' thinking and their engagement with one another. It requires planning, but it also demands improvisation, as teachers must discern during the course of a discussion whether their intervention would support or impede its flow. Perhaps most important of all, it requires that we as teachers rethink our traditional role and transfer certain responsibilities to our students, where they belong.

Mastering quality questioning and using it to engage students in true discussion might seem like a worthwhile but daunting challenge. It is. The good news is, it can be learned. You're already on your way!

Reflecting and Connecting

Questioning for discussion requires teachers to assume a different role from that associated with traditional classroom questioning. In discussion, the teacher typically

- Frames one question to focus the discussion, then questions only when perplexed.
- Refrains from speaking in response to every student comment, leaving space for students to talk to one another.
- Withholds both positive and constructive feedback, allowing students to critique one another's thinking and ideas.

These practices invite teachers to relinquish control and allow students to take their thinking in directions they choose.

How comfortable are you in assuming the above posture during a discussion?

How much of a change would this be from your ordinary practice?

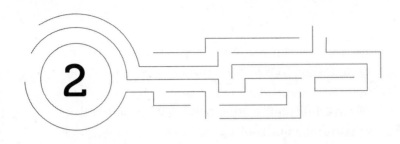

The DNA of Productive Discussion: Social, Cognitive, and Use-of-Knowledge Skills and Companion Dispositions

How can we transform unbridled talk into disciplined discussion?

Students of discussion ascribe certain adjectives to the formal, academic talk associated with this form of discourse, distinguishing it from the more casual, less complex conversation that characterizes most classroom interactions. Primary among these are references to *true* or *authentic* discussion, terms typically used to differentiate group talk driven by critical thinking about an open-ended question from classroom conversation focused on the simple transmission and sharing of information (McCann, 2014; Nystrand, 1997). Others advocate for democratic discussion, which seeks to surface and elicit respect for a diversity of ideas from students who are not seeking to conform to the view of an authority, in this case the teacher (Bridges, 1979; Brookfield & Preskill, 2005; Hess, 2011). These modifiers of discussion suggest that it is widely accepted as an interaction among individuals who are comfortable voicing their views and are open to hearing the ideas of their peers.

Interwoven through this text are other adjectives carefully selected to modify "discussion"—to give definition to our conception of this type of student discourse. At times, we refer to *disciplined* discussion, which we hope conveys talk that follows certain guidelines or procedures. By *thoughtful* discussion, we mean discourse that results from deliberate and intentional thinking. In the previous chapter, we referenced *meaningful* discussion to connote a discussion that is relevant to the student participants and helps them make meaning of the content, which is the raw material for their thinking. We at times speak of *collaborative* discourse, which we envision as the process by which students think together to advance a shared understanding of a topic. At other junctures, we herald *purposeful* discussion, which is intended to convey the importance of discussants understanding and valuing the reason for a given conversation. And in the title of this chapter, we choose to highlight *productive* discussion—conversation that "goes somewhere" and yields an outcome that seems to merit the time dedicated to the discourse. Through use of these adjectives, we convey our view of classroom discussion as follows:

> *Discussion* is a process through which individual students give voice to their thoughts in a disciplined manner as they interact with others to make meaning and advance individual and collective understanding of the issue in question.

If students are to engage in this type of talk, then teachers must nurture and develop student thinking and behavior related to four critical capacities associated with discussion: social skills, cognitive skills, use of knowledge, and dispositions. This chapter presents a framework teachers can use in thinking about how each capacity might shape their practice and expectations for a given group of students. The constituent items in the framework emerge from the literature and state standards and represent a "candidate pool" of discrete competencies that give definition to what teachers might expect of students as they engage in and develop their capacity to discuss.

Our assumption is that most students do not arrive in our classrooms equipped with the skills and dispositions embedded in our framework. Rather, teachers must commit to intentional instruction in the process of discussion.

If students are to learn these skills, they must do so on the practice field of discussion itself. In other words, students learn how to discuss by discussing. Teacher planning of this practice can scaffold the development of student skills in a systematic manner.

It is up to each individual teacher to decide whether he or she thinks classroom discussion, which is a rigorous and demanding type of instruction, is worth the time and effort. Before reading about the student skills and dispositions required for disciplined discussion, pause and take a few minutes to reflect on your own beliefs related to the value of discussion; then read the following paragraphs about teacher beliefs that affect our disposition to engage students in discussion.

Teacher Beliefs Essential to Discussion

Teachers who incorporate discussions into their instructional planning believe that discussion furthers both academic and social/citizenship purposes. However, there are numerous barriers to translating such beliefs into action. One constraint is a lack of personal experience and hence of models for this pedagogical technique. Few of us had opportunities as students to participate in a classroom discussion in which

- Teachers posed questions to prompt and advance student thinking and interaction, rather than to obtain predetermined answers.
- Student voices dominated discourse, and active listening and respect for others' contributions led to the collaborative creation of new perspectives.
- The rhythm and momentum of student-to-student talk sparked energy and excitement for both emerging ideas and the process that yielded them.
- Time stood still as participants sensed being in the flow that Mihaly Csikszentmihalyi describes in his 1990 classic, *Flow: The Psychology of Optimal Experience.*

Absent such an experience, we may not have reflected deeply on either the value of this type of classroom interaction for learners or the core beliefs enabling it to occur. Many of these beliefs run counter to those underpinning traditional classroom discourse and relate to two central issues for teachers: control and time.

Teacher Beliefs About Control

True discussion requires that teachers relinquish some control over both the speaker and the substance and sequence of the ideas that emerge. Implicit in this act is the risk that we may not address or "cover" the exact content we had imagined or that perspectives or interpretations other than our own may emerge—including some based on erroneous information. When the latter occurs, our challenge is to surface the evidence or reasoning that led to a student's incorrect understanding. This requires skill, patience, diplomacy, and time. Many teachers are uncomfortable with this departure from their traditional role, in which the teacher controls who speaks, speaks before and after each student, speaks primarily in questions, and reacts to every student answer by evaluating its value or correctness.

Teacher Beliefs About Time

Other beliefs that frequently pose barriers to our use of discussion relate to time. For example, teachers might believe it's more efficient to tell students what they need to know. According to this line of reasoning, discussion not only takes time away from content coverage but also takes time to plan for appropriate scaffolding within the context of a discussion. Pressures related to pacing guides and high-stakes testing call into question what seems to be a more circuitous way of moving students to deeper or higher levels of understanding.

Reflection on Teacher Beliefs About Discussion

If teachers are to embrace questioning for discussion, we need to confront the issues of time and control. Harnessing both in ways that strengthen student thinking and learning can be extremely difficult for those of us who do not have experience in productive discussion, which is the case for many of us.

Most of our involvement with classroom conversations—as students—was in a setting where the teacher was the fulcrum for all talk and students did not actually engage with one another. Or we may have participated in unbridled classroom discussions that were more a sharing of opinions (or, in some cases, ignorance!) than a search for deeper meaning through a thoughtful exchange of ideas. These experiences might have led to the belief that discussions are a waste of classroom time.

All of us base our beliefs on the inferences we have drawn from our personal experiences. This, according to thought leader Chris Argyris (1990), is rational and normal behavior. Argyris developed a useful tool for reflecting on beliefs—the Ladder of Inferences. In Argyris's view, our beliefs emerge from the conclusions or inferences we draw from assumptions we hold. These assumptions form when we attach meaning to information or data that emerge from our personal experiences. Using beliefs about classroom discussion as the example, we might conclude that discussion is not worth the investment of time because our experiences with this were not positive. We generalized our experiences and developed an assumption that most discussions are wastes of time. Over time, we may have collected more data to substantiate this view, which ultimately became a deeply held belief. (This theory is depicted in Figure 2.1.) Argyris argues that the problem with this practice is that our tendency, once a belief is formed, is to look for reinforcing data rather than stay open to different or even contradictory data that might emanate from new experiences. This is the source of what some call self-fulfilling prophecies: we see what we are looking for and what we currently believe in.

With regard to teacher beliefs about discussion, this preference for information that confirms existing beliefs can translate into a tendency to focus on the downside of true discussion. For instance, if someone believes presentation and recitation are the most efficient ways for students to learn, then that person will not buy into discussion as a valuable mode of instruction. Argyris suggests that we can use the ladder as a tool to reflect on the source of present beliefs and be intentionally open to new situations. If you have colleagues who seem resistant to experimenting with this form of instruction, you may want to use this line of reasoning to uncover their thinking. Perhaps you can use some of the examples provided later in this book to challenge their assumptions.

Figure 2.1 | **Ladder of Inferences**

7. I take actions based on my beliefs.
6. I adopt beliefs.
5. I draw conclusions.
4. I make assumptions.
3. I add meaning from personal experiences.
2. I select "data" on which to focus.
1. I have experiences and make observations that give me data about the world.

Source: Adapted from content found in *Overcoming Organizational Defenses*, by C. Argyris, 1990, Boston: Allyn & Bacon.

The Ladder of Inferences can be useful to teachers in examining their own beliefs. It is also a useful tool for helping students think about how and why they have come to certain positions.

Reflecting and Connecting

Many of us are reticent to integrate true discussions into our unit planning because we do not have confidence in students' abilities to introduce important content into the conversation, or we are concerned that students will not develop the content in appropriate directions. Others have concerns about the amount of time required for a true discussion.

To what extent are you concerned about these issues? Using the Ladder of Inferences, attempt to identify the source of your concerns. What would it take for you to experiment with discussion in your classroom and be open to data that might disconfirm an existing belief or contribute to new ones?

Capacities Required for Productive Discussion

Consider again our conception of discussion as a process through which individual students give voice to their thoughts in a disciplined manner as they interact with others to make meaning and advance individual and collective understanding of the issue in question. Inherent in this view is the assumption that students possess the ability to "give voice to their thoughts in a disciplined manner," which involves both social (speaking and listening) skills and cognitive (thinking) skills. Further embedded in this view is the notion that the extension or deepening of knowledge is a core requirement for the process.

It is safe to say that productive discussion requires skills that students don't necessarily have when they walk through the classroom door. This means teachers will need to determine what skills students currently possess and help them develop identified skill deficits. To assist teachers in making this task manageable, we put productive discussion under the microscope, so to speak, to discover its DNA—the skills and dispositions necessary to build and sustain productive discussion. We identified three skill areas (social skills, cognitive skills, and use of knowledge) and a strand (dispositions related to the skill areas) that is intertwined with the skills. The framework presented in Figure 2.2 is the result of our "genome mapping" work. It highlights various categories of important skills or behaviors associated with discussion and related dispositions. The remainder of this chapter addresses each of these, one by one. A complete listing of the three sets of skills is included in Appendix A.

Social Skills

As Dillon (1994), Bridges (1979), and others suggest, the essence of discussion is its social dimension; it's a process pursued by a group of individuals who focus on a question to anchor their conversation. Dillon suggests that, at its core, discussion involves intentionality in three fundamental acts: speaking, listening, and responding. Three primary skill sets can be associated with the social dimension: speaking, listening, and collaborating.

Speaking. Speaking is a prerequisite to discussion. "Speaking," as used here, is a more formal and intentional form of communication than "talking."

Figure 2.2 | **Capacities Associated with Skilled Discussion**

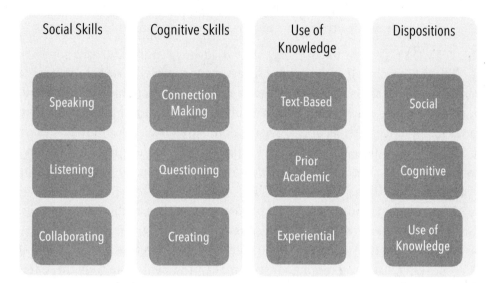

Speaking connotes attention to both the form and substance of the communication. Certain speaking skills are prerequisite to a productive discussion. The following foundational skills pertain to the manner in which the speaker articulates and directs comments.

- Speaks clearly and loudly enough that everyone can hear.
- Speaks when there is an opening in the discussion, without raising a hand.
- Speaks to classmates as well as to the teacher.
- Speaks in complete sentences.
- Contributes to the discussion so everyone can learn from him or her.

Although these skills seem relatively simple, they are counter to what usually occurs in classrooms. As teachers, we must be explicit about our expectations for these behaviors and provide students with opportunities for practice with feedback. Students can begin learning these skills from their first years in school.

Other speaking skills are more dependent on a student's knowledge of the content under discussion and on their ability to think about this content.

- Expresses own ideas clearly.
- Speaks at length so that thinking is visible to others.
- Paraphrases portions of a text or information presented in other formats.

The skills included in the second set are more complex. They are standards-based, academic skills. Most students do not arrive at school with proficiency in these skills. Teachers need to model, offer exemplars, and provide opportunities for practice with feedback. Discussion is the ideal forum for practice of these skills. As students practice and refine the skills, they develop the confidence required to become better discussants. In turn, the quality of classroom discussions improves.

Listening. Listening is the companion to speaking in the CCSS, and it is the critical partner to speaking if a discussion is to occur. Even as speaking can be distinguished from talking, so can listening be differentiated from hearing. Like speaking, listening requires intentionality and deliberate thought. Often, when students appear to be paying attention, they are hearing but not really listening. Listening is difficult to observe in and of itself. The core skill of listening, particularly in discussion, is that our students actively listen to understand what is behind a classmate's words—to uncover what the speaker means. The following behaviors provide clues that a student is actively listening. Each of these is a skill that teachers can model for students; each is also a skill that teachers can observe:

- Uses silence after a classmate stops speaking to think about what the speaker said and to compare the speaker's thinking to one's own.
- Asks questions to better understand the speaker's point of view.
- Waits before adding one's own ideas to ensure that the speaker has completed his or her thoughts.
- Accurately paraphrases what another student says.
- Looks at the speaking student and gives nonverbal cues that one is paying attention.

Collaborating. A true discussion is more like a game of soccer than of ping-pong or tennis. Students build upon one another's ideas as they seek to expand their individual and collective understandings. Discussion occurs when the field of play includes all discussants, not just a select few who "hit the ball" back and forth among themselves, excluding most of their classmates. In a successful discussion, students truly engage in joint inquiry, shared deliberation, and mutual consideration. So, beyond individual speaking and listening, discussion requires students to develop and use skills of collaboration. Like speaking and listening skills, some collaborative skills are relatively simple and observable, if not habitual, behaviors for students. They are no less important for the unfolding of a productive discussion.

- "Piggybacks" and elaborates on classmates' comments.
- Actively seeks to include classmates who are not participating.
- Responds to classmates' questions nondefensively.

A true discussion is more like a game of soccer than of ping-pong or tennis.

Other collaborative skills are more complex and less observable, and they seem closely tied to dispositions. These skills, critical to civil discourse, are needed by students for productive participation in our democratic society.

- Remains open to ideas that are different from one's own.
- Actively seeks to understand and communicate with individuals who have different backgrounds and perspectives.
- Disagrees in a civil and respectful manner.

How can teachers help students develop these skills, which are essential to discussion? Again, teacher modeling can be powerful. Teachers can intentionally and routinely use language associated with the skill they are encouraging students to develop—and call student attention to "discussant" behaviors. Teachers might use consistent stems or lead-ins, such as those in Figure 2.3, and share these with students by presenting them on anchor charts or handouts. Additionally, teachers might ask their students what language they would use, for example, to disagree with someone's idea while also communicating respect for the individual.

Figure 2.3 | **Scaffolding Students' Development of Collaborative Skills for Discussion**

Skill	Stem
Elaborates on classmate's ideas	• I want to piggyback on what [student name] said earlier. • I'd like to build on what [student name] said. • [Student name] reminded me of . . . • [Student name] reinforced what I believe about . . . • I appreciate what [student name] said and want to add to it.
Actively seeks to include classmates who are not participating	• I am wondering what you are thinking about this, [classmate's name]. • I've been talking a lot, and I'm curious as to what others are thinking.
Responds to classmates' questions and rebuttals nondefensively	• You pose a very good question. This is how I arrived at my thinking. • Let me clarify my thinking. You may not agree with me, but I'd like you to understand my point of view.
Remains open to ideas that are different from one's own	• I hadn't thought of it in this way, but I wonder . . . • This is not what I was thinking, but I'd like to hear more about how you arrived at this position. • I've been thinking of this differently, but want to suspend judgment and hear from others who are thinking this way.
Actively seeks to understand a different point of view	• Can you tell me more about your point of view? • This is a different way of thinking from mine. Can you help me understand what makes you say this? • I have a question about what [student name] said: [Pose question].
Disagrees in a respectful manner	• I respect what [student name] is saying, but I want to offer a different perspective. • I am thinking about this differently and want to put my idea in the mix. • Perhaps we'll have to agree to disagree, but I wonder if we have the same understanding of the definition or the meaning of this word. • I hear what [student name] is saying. I want to offer a different interpretation. • I've heard several different perspectives. I want to add yet another one.

Cognitive Skills

Students certainly must think in order to speak, listen, and collaborate with intentionality. Discussions, however, challenge students to think more deeply as they engage with knowledge related to the question under discussion in cognitively complex ways. Discussion is an arena in which students must use higher-level cognitive skills to develop or enhance understandings, reach judgments, or create new ways of thinking.

Most teachers will agree that cognitive processing skills present the greatest challenges to student mastery of new standards, whether they are CCSS or other current state standards. It is for this reason that important cognitive skills are repeated in the CCSS across the three components of literacy: reading, speaking and listening, and writing. For example, anchor standards in all three of these components call for students to integrate and evaluate information:

- **Reading:** Integrate and evaluate content presented in diverse media and formats, including visually and quantitatively, as well as in words. (CCSS.ELA-Literacy.CCRA.R.7)
- **Speaking and Listening:** Integrate and evaluate information presented in diverse media and formats, including visually, quantitatively, and orally. (CCSS.ELA-Literacy.CCRA.SL.2)
- **Writing:** Gather relevant information from multiple print and digital sources, assess the credibility and accuracy of each source, and integrate the information while avoiding plagiarism. (CCSS.ELA-Literacy.CCRA.SL.2)

While developing students' skills evaluating, integrating, and synthesizing information, teachers can incorporate student reading assignments into the planning for a given discussion and connect writing assignments to the reading and discussion. Discussions are the practice fields for cognitive skills that span all three components of literacy. For example, teachers can use text to point out how an author integrated and evaluated sources and then ask students to use these same operations in a short written piece to prepare for classroom discourse. It is in discussion, however, that students truly experience what "evaluate" feels and sounds like in practice as they engage with classmates and consider an issue of importance. A well-planned discussion can engage students in authentic dialogue that requires them to evaluate not only texts but also one another's ideas. Discussion also allows students to build on one another's thoughts to better synthesize ideas. Following a discussion, individual students are often better able to independently evaluate and integrate information in writing—and in real-life situations.

To engage in and sustain the thinking required for discussion, students must undertake three distinct types of cognitive operations: connection making, questioning, and creating.

Connection making. We define *connection making* as the thinking that students carry out as they make deeper meaning and (1) connect their own ideas to those of others, (2) connect their prior knowledge to the focus of the discussion, (3) connect their personal experience and knowledge to a specific text or other source under consideration, and (4) link or integrate ideas from two or more different texts or other sources. The list, of course, goes on. Many of the cognitive skills associated with connection making appear in the CCSS and state standards. Teachers can help students understand that connection making is an important part of thinking and discussing. Some key cognitive skills associated with connection making include the following:

- Identifies similarities and differences between one's own ideas and those of others.
- Relates prior knowledge (both academic and personal) to the topic of discussion.
- Offers reasons and textual evidence to support one's own point of view.
- Analyzes and evaluates information from different sources.

As students make connections, they extend and deepen their understanding of the core concepts embedded in the discussion.

Questioning. Student questioning is essential to a lively, thoughtful discussion. Without student questions, there can be no joint or shared inquiry. Without student questions, there is no real evidence of student curiosity. In a thoughtful discussion, students direct their questions to three sources: the content or focus for discussion, other discussants, and themselves. First, their questions give voice to their puzzlements or curiosity about the issue or topic under discussion. For example, they might have questions about the source materials or questions that arise from their own out-of-school experiences. Second, they question one another as they listen to and seek to understand others' perspectives or points of view. Third, they might question some of their own beliefs or positions. Thoughtful discussants need to develop the following skills related to question asking:

- Poses questions to clarify and better understand the substance of a topic or text.
- Asks questions to identify a speaker's assumptions.
- Poses questions to clarify the thinking or reasoning behind an argument or conclusion.
- Surfaces and questions own assumptions.
- Asks questions when curious.
- Asks "what if" questions to encourage divergent thinking.

Chapters 3 and 4 address how teachers can support student development of these skills through modeling, scaffolding, and coaching, and they provide tools teachers and students can use in the process. (In particular, see Figure 3.4 on page 97.)

Creating. The highest form of discussion occurs when student interactions lead to new insights, understandings, interpretations, or solutions. Such creative thinking stands on the shoulders of solid connection making and questioning. It does not occur in a vacuum but emerges from the deep understandings and evaluations that emerge when students make connections and ask questions. The ideas that result clearly differ from student "opinions" that are frequently voiced during student discussions. Creation calls upon students to use the "integration" skills featured in the CCSS. Integration or synthesis of knowledge is usually a prerequisite to creation. This supports breakthrough thinking that leads to a new way of looking at a topic or issue.

Discussion provides an environment that allows students to work collaboratively to weave ideas together to create new patterns. Collaborative thinking is a key to innovation. Walter Isaacson (2014) highlights the importance of "the collaborative spirit" to advances in the digital age. The collaborative spirit is no less important to advances in student learning as students think together in classroom settings.

Creation relies on cognitive skills that enable students to go beyond "the givens" in a text or other information source. Hallmarks of the creative impulse in discussions include the following qualities:

- Draws inferences from different speakers' ideas that take the conversation to a deeper level.
- Integrates information from multiple sources to produce a new way of thinking.
- Suspends judgment while listening to a new solution or interpretation from a classmate.
- Contributes to the building of collaborative solutions.

Students develop and refine the cognitive skills outlined throughout this section as they use the social skills previously presented. It is the conjoining of the social and cognitive skills that produces the opportunity for a discussion focused on a shared question about a particular topic. Knowledge provides students with the essential raw material for this process.

Use of Knowledge

The type of classroom discussion we imagine is not a sharing of opinions, which is the experience many associate with student discussion. Rather, it is a disciplined discourse in which students—exercising skills associated with speaking, listening, and collaborating—use appropriate cognitive skills to manipulate knowledge related to the question under discussion. A robust discussion requires that participants access a diverse and deep knowledge base. We identify three spheres of knowledge that students may draw from as they address a shared question: text-based knowledge, prior academic knowledge, and experiential knowledge.

Discussion offers a unique opportunity for students to connect information across these three spheres as teachers challenge them to integrate academic knowledge with their individual worldviews. Further, it provides an arena in which students can use this knowledge to deepen their understanding of a text. In this way, discussion becomes a laboratory in which students grapple with and "test" individual and collective understandings of knowledge related to a shared question. The following skills apply to all three spheres of knowledge:

- Strives for accuracy in the presentation of facts.
- Cites information sources.
- Evaluates the credibility of information sources.
- Relates comments to the subject or question for discussion; does not get off topic.

Careful selection of pre-discussion readings or research assignments is perhaps the most important step teachers can take as they assist students in improving their ability to access and use knowledge through discussion. In Chapters 3–5, we address pre-discussion assignments in connection with the planning stage of discussion. When students and the teacher share common ground for discussion in the form of a shared reading, their discourse is likely to be more connected. This does not preclude students from undertaking independent research prior to a discussion; however, we believe that all discussants should read at least one common source related to the focus question prior to a discussion. If we fail to hold students accountable for preparation, the discourse is at risk of getting mired down or going off course. Knowledge centers a discussion, and shared knowledge provides a point of departure for different interpretations and perspectives.

Teacher review of expectations or skills related to the use of knowledge is a second form of support that teachers provide prior to the discussion itself. In our view, the four skills we identified are universal. They are appropriate for students at all developmental stages, and they are important in all discussions across all disciplines. They are worthy of posting, perhaps on an anchor chart, to keep them at the forefront of student and teacher consciousness.

Figure 2.4 provides prompts and stems that teachers can employ during discussion to support students' skillful use of knowledge. Students can also refer to these stems as they learn to assume responsibility for supporting and holding one another accountable during a discussion.

Figure 2.4 | **Scaffolding Students' Development of Use-of-Knowledge Skills for Discussion**

Skill	Stems and Prompts
Strives for accuracy in presentation of facts	• I'm wondering where you found this information. • Could you repeat the [facts, chain of events, steps, etc.] that led you to this [conclusion, solution]? You seem to have omitted a step.
Cites information sources	• I'm wondering about the source for this . . . • Where did you locate this information?
Evaluates the credibility of information sources	• What can you tell us about this information source? • Who was the publisher of this piece? or Who is the sponsor of this website? • Who are the authors of this text? What do you know about them? What are their credentials? or What institution supported this work? What do you know about this organization? • What gives you confidence in this publication, website, or information source? • Was this a scholarly article, or did it come from the popular press? • To what extent does the author appear to present an objective and balanced account of the topic? • When was this site [or publication] last updated? Is all of the information still accurate?
Relates comments to the subject or question for discussion; does not get off topic	• We have been discussing _____. Can you relate your comment to this topic? • I cannot make the connection between your comment and the focus question for our discussion. I'd like to get behind your thinking.
Integrates evidence from multiple sources into one's argument	• You've provided relevant information from one source. Can you connect the ideas of [another author] to what you just said? • How would you relate the ideas of _____ to your argument?
Uses information that is relevant to the discussion topic and focus question	• How does [the comment or idea presented] relate to our focus question? • I'm interested in how you are connecting your comment to the focus question [or to an idea previously presented].

Scaffolding of this set of skills through the use of prompts is a delicate but essential task. In Chapter 1, we suggested that teacher feedback can shut down student thinking and speaking and break the rhythm of student-to-student talk. When teachers provide feedback, they take control from their students and revert, at least in the eyes of students, to being "the expert."

Therefore, scaffolding use-of-knowledge skills requires teachers to walk a fine line between supporting students and providing direct corrective feedback.

For example, when students draw from a text that is extremely biased, it is tempting to tell them that they are using an inappropriate source; however, it is more productive to have the students themselves reflect on their sources and learn how to evaluate them. Hence, we suggest using comments or questions such as those offered in Figure 2.4. This is a delicate area requiring a great deal of teacher skill and discretion.

Likewise, when a student's comment threatens to take the discussion in an unproductive direction, it is tempting to simply state, "Your comments are off topic." At first blush, this student comment may have seemed to be completely unrelated to the discussion; however, when given an opportunity to develop the idea, the student and other classmates may either make connections to the topic at hand or legitimize the comment as fertile ground for this or future discussions. Alternatively, other students may ask the speaker about the relationship of the comment to the discussion. When appropriate, the teacher may respectfully invite the student to reflect on his or her statement and consider if and how it connects to the focus of the discussion.

Beyond the four expectations or skills that students are expected to apply to all information brought to the discussion table, special conditions and expectations are unique to each sphere of knowledge. Students need to understand how various domains of knowledge can potentially contribute to a discussion. They also need to understand teacher expectations related to each.

Text-based knowledge. One of the hallmarks of current standards is an emphasis on students' ability to understand, analyze, and make inferences from texts and use textual evidence to support their positions when speaking and writing. Teachers are increasingly planning and facilitating discussions during which students have a text in hand and are ready to point others to the page and line related to their comments. Likewise, students can engage in similar analysis of a piece of visual art, a work of music, or a product from other fields to identify evidence that supports their positions. The ability to effectively analyze and draw from a text or other source during a discussion requires students to have a number of skills.

- Evidences serious preparation for discussion by referring to texts and related research or to other media (e.g., a work from visual art or music).
- Cites specific evidence from text or other source.
- Integrates evidence from multiple texts or sources into one's argument.
- Uses academic vocabulary and the language of the discipline.

Prior academic knowledge. Discussion offers teachers and students the opportunity to connect knowledge from various disciplines or from previous learning to information gleaned from assigned texts. This is a valuable function, as learning in school can seem fragmented to students moving from unit to unit and subject to subject across a school day and term (Perkins, 2010). If students are to develop their own mental frames and ways of thinking, they need more experience in "putting the pieces together." A primary purpose of discussion is to provide an arena in which students can integrate information in meaningful ways, thereby developing a more holistic worldview. Depending on the purpose and frame for a particular discussion, teachers can encourage students to draw ideas from across a discipline and between and among different disciplines. The way teachers frame a question for discussion can encourage or discourage this type of connection making. Again, students must know our expectations for them in this area.

- Draws relevant information from prior learning in the subject area (discipline) under study.
- Draws relevant information from other subject areas.

Experiential knowledge. A large part of a student's knowledge base consists of information learned outside school. Discussion is a forum in which students can connect academic knowledge to that derived from "real life." When students inject this type of information into a discussion, they are better able to discern the relevance of school learning to real life. When bringing this type of information to the fore, it is particularly important that students are able to judge the relevance and appropriateness of potential contributions to the question for discussion.

- Introduces relevant information from out-of-school sources.
- Reflects on and evaluates personal beliefs or positions on issues in relation to ideas offered in a discussion.
- Connects current social, economic, or cultural phenomena to academic content on which a discussion is focused.
- Assesses appropriateness of information to the classroom arena.

Dispositions That Support Productive Discussion

Student skills are not sufficient for vibrant, productive discussions; certain dispositions must also be in play. If skills are the yin of discussion, then dispositions are the yang.

If skills are the yin of discussion, then dispositions are the yang.

The simple definition of *disposition* is "the tendency to think or act in a particular way." Costa and Kallick (2014) suggest that thinking dispositions are "tendencies toward particular patterns of intellectual behavior" (p. 19). They cite the contributions of Paul Ennis to their thinking "that the disposition must be exercised reflectively. In other words, given the appropriate conditions, dispositions are not automatic."

Dispositions cannot be assumed; they must be made explicit and taught to students. Students, in turn, must be mindful of dispositions as they interact with one another and with their environment.

Identifying dispositions for discussion. Dillon (1994), in his classic *Using Discussion in Classrooms,* identifies "moral dispositions" that he sees as critical for discussion: "reasonableness, peaceableness and orderliness, truthfulness, freedom, equality, and respect for persons" (pp. 9–10). Additionally, Dillon suggests other intellectual qualities that are critical to the success of discussion, such as "respect for the opinions of others," responsiveness, judiciousness, reflectiveness, and evidence (pp. 10–11). Most important, perhaps, he focuses on "the disposition to discuss . . . a basic willingness to talk things over with other people," which "embraces as a matter of course a series of other sentiments or attitudes such as open-mindedness, reasonableness, respect for other opinions, and the like" (p. 45).

Costa and Kallick (2014) identify 12 dispositions that they claim to be research-based. We can imagine all of them being important to productive discussion: perseverance; managing impulsivity; questioning; finding wonderment and awe; listening with understanding and empathy; drawing on prior knowledge and applying it to new situations; being adventuresome; risk taking; creating, imagining, and innovating; striving for craftsmanship; using clear and precise language; and metacognition (thinking about thinking).

Other authors who advocate for discussion suggest the need for similar dispositions (Brookfield & Preskill, 2005; Hale & City, 2006; Haroutunian-Gordon, 2014; McCann 2014). Figure 2.5 presents the dispositions we have found to be of greatest importance to the success of discussion across all grade levels and content areas. As we classified these dispositions, we discovered that they sorted nicely into three categories that mirror the three identified skill areas.

The relationship between the three skill sets and the three categories of dispositions is no accident. If students are to be intentional in developing a given skill, they must have an underlying propensity to act in that manner. As we teach students identified skills, we can also teach them corresponding dispositions.

As you further examine Figure 2.5, you might also notice that a number of dispositions are identical to certain skills. Active listening, for example, appears as both a skill and a disposition. As previously noted, one cannot directly observe active listening—only the clues that it is occurring, such as students making eye contact, taking notes, or conveying their interest in some other nonverbal way. We believe there must first be the disposition to listen actively, which we can only surmise, before specific and concrete behaviors associated with active listening can be performed. Similarly, we list open-mindedness as both a social skill and a disposition. As with active listening, the tendency to be open to a conflicting view must be present before related skills can be

Figure 2.5 | **Dispositions Associated with Skillful Discussants**

Disposition	What It Looks Like During Discussion
Social	
Active Listening	Students listen to understand others' points of view. They look at the speaker with interest; think about what the speaker is saying; and question to get behind what they may not, at first, understand.
Open-mindedness	Students listen to others and ask questions with a genuine interest in another's point of view. They are open to continual learning about a topic.
Managing Impulsivity	Students think before speaking. They suspend judgment and reflect on their initial reactions. They seek to uncover all of the evidence, and they listen to a speaker's reasoning to its culmination.
Cognitive	
Perseverance or Persistence	Students do not give up when confronting a difficult topic; rather, they redouble their efforts and "stay the course," thinking deeply and interacting with classmates to deepen understanding.
Taking Reasonable Risks	Students are adventuresome in their thinking. They are willing to move outside the bounds of certainty to offer a new solution to a problem or to introduce a new topic for investigation. They are not afraid to venture into new territories of thinking and learning. They understand that we all learn from our mistakes.
Flexibility in Thinking	Students are willing to "try out" different types of thinking and different points of view. They are open to the influence of others' thinking.
Reasonableness	Students value evidence and logic. They subject their own thinking to this standard and seek to uncover evidence and logic in the positions of their peers.
Reflectiveness	Students value time to think about hard questions and issues, as well as their own stance in an argument, and the quality of their thinking and speaking.
Use of Knowledge	
Striving for Accuracy	Students provide or seek evidence to support their conclusions. They reflect on their thinking to self-assess and self-correct.
Applying Prior Knowledge to New Situations	Students activate prior knowledge and transfer it to new situations.

exercised. Striving for accuracy, implicit in a number of the knowledge-related indicators, also made both the skills and dispositions lists for similar reasons.

Developing student dispositions for discussion. Like others who have written about discussion, we hold the conviction that shared dispositions are essential to productive discussion. The following guidelines can help teachers decide which dispositions are important to them and their students and how to help students develop these habits of mind.

- Identify a limited number of dispositions you believe will be most important to your students as they form a community of discussants. As a starting point, we recommend no more than three to five, depending on the age and maturity of the group. You may wish to think of how you would phase in additional dispositions as the group matures.
- Be explicit with students about the "what" and "why" of dispositions. Help students understand the importance of thinking and acting in particular ways as they talk with (and learn from) one another.
- Introduce one disposition at a time, creating opportunities for students to learn academic vocabulary and to engage in mini-discussions about what a particular disposition might look, sound, and feel like.
- Make the dispositions public. Create wall or anchor charts to display the dispositions—or have students make these.
- Intentionally model the dispositions, naming each as you demonstrate it. For example, you might say, "It was hard for me to keep from interrupting earlier because I really wanted to say what I was thinking. But I know it's important for me to manage my impulsivity, to think before I speak, and to wait until others have finished."
- Encourage students to self-assess their use of agreed-upon dispositions following a discussion and to think about if and how the ways of thinking are becoming more natural to them.
- Periodically evaluate where each of your classes is in their use of agreed-upon dispositions. Determine whether you need to add or otherwise modify a given class's set of dispositions.

Dispositions in general, and the specific dispositions included in Figure 2.5, would be good topics for discussion. We can imagine asking pairs of students to "make a case" for why a particular disposition is important to productive classroom talk. The initial discussion could ensue within each pair. The pairs could then share their thoughts with the whole group, and other students could be invited to respond with questions or comments.

Toward Disciplined Discussion

Students' ability to apply the various skills of productive discussion—social, cognitive, and use of knowledge—along with related dispositions, enable them to engage in a relevant, meaningful, and significant discussion. When students receive explicit instruction in these skills and dispositions, and when teachers craft quality questions to focus students' attention, discussion can be a dynamic way for students to deepen their understanding of academic knowledge and gain important life skills while meeting state standards. Our vision for a productive discussion is one of students as potters who collaboratively mold the clay—or knowledge—into multiple, beautiful forms. The magic of discussion is that we, the teachers, never know what shapes or colors will emerge.

It can't be assumed that students already have the knowledge, skills, or dispositions to do this work. Neither can it be assumed that these things can't be learned. They must be developed over time, as teachers scaffold the development of new attitudes and behaviors while engaging students in a variety of teacher-guided, structured small-group, and student-driven discussion formats. The next three chapters explore these forms of discussion.

Although we describe the skills and dispositions presented here as the DNA of productive discussion, we do not claim that this compendium is all-inclusive. Nor do we suggest that all of these skills and dispositions are appropriate for all content areas or grade levels. Teachers will need to use their professional judgment to select the strands most appropriate to their particular context and students.

Reflecting and Connecting

Think about the three sets of skills for discussion presented in this chapter: social, cognitive, and use of knowledge.

- *Which skill set do you feel is the best starting point for your students, given their age and developmental level?*
- *Which skill set do you believe might be the most challenging for your students to learn and practice?*
- *What are some possible benefits of collaborating with colleagues to determine which of these skills to focus on with students in your school?*

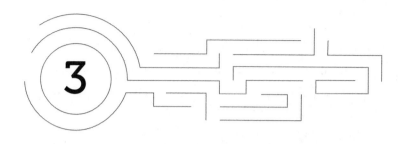

Teacher-Guided Discussion: Teachers as Coaches During Five Stages of Discussion

In what ways can we intentionally and explicitly model skills and dispositions, scaffold thinking, and coach students to become effective participants in discussions?

In teacher-guided discussions, teachers strategically engage and instruct students in classroom conversation while deepening their understanding of content. Within the arena of teacher-guided discussion, students become apprentices to their teachers as they develop and refine skills for productive and disciplined discussion.

The keys to an effective teacher-guided discussion are teacher intentionality and explicitness. *Intentionality* relates to teacher decision making about which discussion skills will be the primary foci for student development during a given teacher-guided discussion. Teachers make this decision as they prepare for a discussion prior to the class period in which it will occur. They thoughtfully decide when they expect to model which skills as the discussion unfolds. *Explicitness* means teachers "thinking aloud" with students as they intentionally highlight certain skills, dispositions, and productive discussion moves. During the opening of a discussion, the teacher informs students of the specific discussion skills they will be working on and why these skills are important to a disciplined discussion. As the discussion ensues, the teacher continues to call attention to these skills and related dispositions that sustain productive interaction. When teachers are intentional and explicit, they use modeling, scaffolding, and coaching to teach the social, cognitive, and use-of-knowledge skills that students need for disciplined discussion.

Modeling, Scaffolding, and Coaching

Modeling is particularly important in developing the skills and dispositions presented in the previous chapter. For example, a teacher who intentionally focuses on the dispositions of active listening and controlling impulsivity, along with skills associated with active listening, might list these dispositions and skills for all to see. During the discussion, after a prolonged silence, the teacher can refer students to the list while making his or her thinking explicit:

> I used the silence after you stopped speaking to think about what you said and to compare it to my thinking. When I wait before reacting to what someone says, I'm better able to consider that person's point of view—and to decide if I understand or if I need to ask a question to clarify the speaker's intended meaning. You know it's sometimes difficult for me to keep from blurting out what I'm thinking even before a speaker completes his or her thoughts. But when I remember to use this silence, it reminds me to listen actively and helps me control my impulsivity.

This type of teacher modeling does not usually occur spontaneously but requires forethought. We suggest that as part of planning for a given discussion, teachers identify a limited number of discrete skills on which to focus. During this discussion, teachers can then be particularly mindful of modeling these skills and of being very explicit with students about what they are doing.

Teachers routinely use scaffolding to develop student understanding and mastery of content under study. Scaffolding of content knowledge and skills is sometimes appropriate during teacher-guided discussion; however, it is the scaffolding of discussion skills that is our focus in this chapter. When teachers tailor their questions or comments to support students in sharpening their thinking, they are scaffolding student development of expertise in using one or more cognitive skills. For example, imagine that a class is focusing on the following cognitive skill: offers reasons and textual evidence to support one's own point of view. Further imagine that a student has just offered an opinion regarding the morality of a character in a short story. Teacher scaffolding might be as simple as this: "You seem to believe that John is dishonest. I'm interested in the textual evidence you have to support this view." The teacher points to the cognitive skill posted on the board and continues, "Where in the story can you find evidence to support your view that John is dishonest?" As with modeling, the teacher is intentional and explicit as she offers this support. Teacher scaffolding is a core practice in sustaining individual and group thinking and speaking during discussion. Later in this chapter, we offer multiple alternative teacher moves that can serve to scaffold and thereby sustain a discussion.

Modeling and scaffolding are invaluable ways for teachers to assist students in becoming more effective participants. Although these functions are associated with coaching, coaching involves much more. As students learn the skills of discussion, it is sometimes necessary to stop the flow of conversation—to take a time-out—and provide direct instruction in a particular skill. Consider a 3rd grade teacher who intervenes into a class discussion about *Charlotte's Web* to ask students how their thinking about Mr. Arable's motives for moving Wilbur outside compares to a classmate's. When one student responds, "I think I kinda agree and I kinda disagree," the teacher asks, "What do you agree with?" The student shrugs her shoulders. The teacher invites other students to respond. They are silent. The class is working on a cognitive skill: identifying similarities and differences between own and others' ideas.

The teacher introduces a graphic organizer to help students make their thinking visible, directing students to the text and prompting them to find references relevant to Mr. Arable's motives. With the teacher's guidance, the class completes the graphic organizer, placing textual evidence that supports the original speaker's position in one box and evidence that might be used to support a different point of view in another. The teacher then restates the original speaker's position about Mr. Arable's motives and asks the class to talk about what they think. Three students respond to the question. When talk stops, the teacher asks the entire class to think back on how the use of a graphic organizer to share similarities and differences in thinking about Mr. Arable's motives helped move the discussion forward—and how it helped them clarify their thinking about this part of the story. This type of teacher intervention is comparable to a coach calling for a time-out during the course of a game for the purpose of giving players specific guidance designed to improve performance.

Intentional and explicit teacher modeling, scaffolding, and coaching are invaluable to students as they learn to interact with one another and with academic content in productive ways. This is particularly true for young students and for those new to discussions. If we teachers are to assume this "master" role in developing the discussion skills among our student apprentices, we must believe in the value of inducting our students into this form of discourse by demonstrating certain dispositions and proactively planning for the discussions we guide.

Critical Teacher Habits of Mind

All participants need certain dispositions in order to participate in productive discussion. Teachers need to actively model the dispositions discussed in this chapter for their students. Furthermore, teachers need to adopt certain habits of mind that will enable them to exhibit the attitudes and behaviors they want to develop in their student apprentices. Four habits of mind are critical.

Appreciative Listening

Listening appreciatively means listening both actively to understand the student speaker's thinking and empathically to relate to the feelings behind the speaker's words. To do this, a teacher must allow the student's comment to occupy the space and time required for everyone to grapple with its meaning. Use of silence, or "think time," plays an important role. This is especially true when the substantive nature of a comment is mediated by the speaker's emotion. Giving attention to both words and feelings enables the teacher to respond appropriately—either to ensure tolerance or to defuse a potentially negative situation.

Teachers exhibit appreciative listening not only through attentiveness but also by remembering a student's specific contributions so they can refer back to them later, either during the discussion or when providing formal or informal feedback.

Valuing Student Contributions

Appreciative listening is a first step in communicating to students that we value their thinking and contributions. However, valuing also involves an authentic, sincere regard for the student who is attempting to make a positive contribution to the discussion. We demonstrate such regard by maintaining eye contact, nodding, or otherwise demonstrating our engagement with the student and his or her thinking. In addition, we respond respectfully to students even when helping them work through poorly conceived points of view.

Focused Thinking

As we give attention to students, we must keep the focus question (and the learning target that it advances) in the front of our minds. This is critical if we are to maintain the integrity and coherence of a discussion—and provide skillful scaffolding during "real time" in a class discussion. Teachers also want to keep the targeted skills front and center for their own and their students' attention.

Fair-mindedness

Objective, even-handed responses to student comments convey neither favoritism nor negativity toward individual students and encourage everyone to participate in discussions. One strategy for assuming an objective stance is to withhold feedback unless a student uses erroneous information or faulty reasoning. Because the traditional role teachers play in classrooms is that of an expert and authority figure rather than a coach or mentor, actively conveying a fair-minded stance is essential to encouraging student participation in discussions.

Without these four habits of mind—appreciative listening, valuing student contributions, focused thinking, and fair-mindedness—teachers have neither the spark to light the engine of discussion nor the energy to sustain it. These habits constitute a mind-set for nurturing true discussion. When they guide our interactions with students, students are more likely to embrace the dispositions we expect of them and to develop the skills required for productive interactions.

The Discussion Cycle: A Framework for Teacher-Guided Discussions

Good discussions don't just happen. They happen because teachers plan and students prepare. Systematic planning enables teachers to be intentional and explicit as they guide students in developing the skills and dispositions for productive discussion. To plan and lead a successful teacher-guided discussion, teachers need to consider five distinct stages of the discussion process (see Figure 3.1).

These stages are important in structured small-group discussions and student-driven discussions as well as in teacher-guided discussions. However, the planning for teacher-guided discussions is more extensive, particularly during the sustaining stage, because of the need to be intentional and explicit.

Preparing

Preparing for a productive classroom discussion involves five key tasks. The first four affect the substance and quality of ideas that will emerge through student interactions. The last one is organizational and can affect the quality of the interactions themselves.

Frame the focus question for discussion. The quality of the focus question is an important determinant of the quality of the discussion. Therefore, the first task in preparing for a teacher-guided discussion is to frame a focus question that will drive discussion. This requires thoughtful consideration of the content and form of the question. In Chapter 1, we looked at steps teachers

Figure 3.1 | **Stages of the Discussion Process**

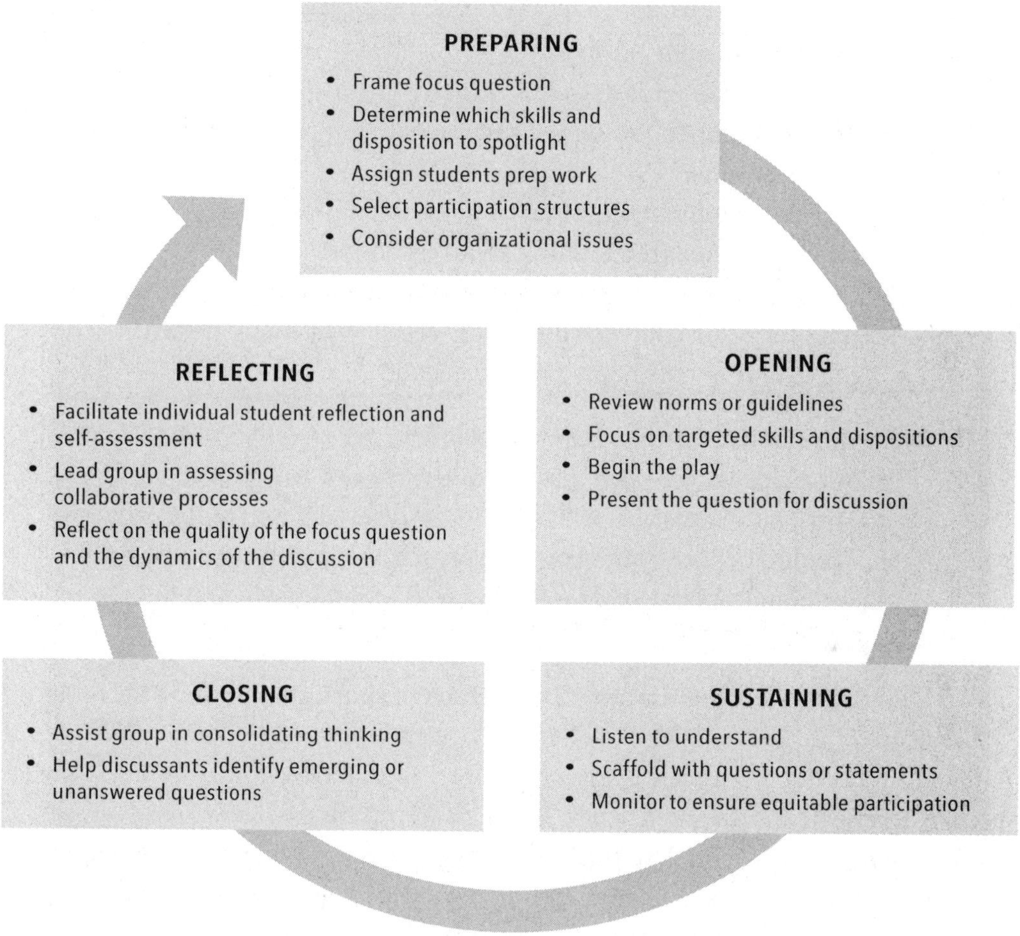

PREPARING
- Frame focus question
- Determine which skills and disposition to spotlight
- Assign students prep work
- Select participation structures
- Consider organizational issues

REFLECTING
- Facilitate individual student reflection and self-assessment
- Lead group in assessing collaborative processes
- Reflect on the quality of the focus question and the dynamics of the discussion

OPENING
- Review norms or guidelines
- Focus on targeted skills and dispositions
- Begin the play
- Present the question for discussion

CLOSING
- Assist group in consolidating thinking
- Help discussants identify emerging or unanswered questions

SUSTAINING
- Listen to understand
- Scaffold with questions or statements
- Monitor to ensure equitable participation

can take in framing a high-quality focus question, underscoring the importance of building the question around an issue that is complex or controversial enough to engage students in deep thinking. In addition, making an academic concept important or relevant to a particular group of students is essential to writing questions that "work" in discussion. The questions presented here can assist in framing a powerful focus question.

Framing the Focus Question for Discussion

A. Issue or Key Concept
- To which standards does this relate?
- To what extent does the issue invite multiple perspectives or points of view?
- To what extent do the students possess the breadth and depth of knowledge required to think about the issue?
- In what ways might this issue engage students? To what extent does the issue relate to student interests? Why might it seem important or relevant to these students?

B. Wording and Structure of the Question
- What academic vocabulary is embedded in the question?
- What verb (or verbs) will activate the desired depth of thinking?
- Would a context-setting preamble, such as a lead-in sentence, help focus and activate student thinking? If so, what might that be?

Determine which skills and dispositions to spotlight. Limiting the number of social, cognitive, and use-of-knowledge skills and dispositions to be targeted in a given discussion is essential. The key criterion is this: *What is the current level of student proficiency, based on formative feedback from previous classroom conversations?* Use this tool to assist in identifying the most appropriate skills and dispositions to target for a particular group of students during a given discussion. (See Chapter 2 for details about a wide range of skills and dispositions.)

Selecting Discussion Skills and Dispositions

A. Social Skills. Consider your students' current proficiencies in speaking, listening, and collaborative thinking. If most students in your class have *not* mastered these fundamental social skills, the primary focus for this

discussion should be on social skills. If most of your students demon-strate mastery of core social skills, select up to three of these for review and reinforcement—and target skills from the other categories.
    1.
    2.
    3.

B. Cognitive Skills. Examine the focus question to help you decide which cognitive skills to target. Consider (1) the verbs in the focus question and (2) probable student responses. Select a limited number of cogni-tive skills, and be prepared to model them through think-alouds.
    1.
    2.

C. Use-of-Knowledge Skills. Examine the focus question to help you decide which use-of-knowledge skills to target. For example, to what extent does the focus question invite students to integrate information from other disciplines or out-of-school experiences—or to access and evaluate multiple sources?
    1.
    2.

D. Dispositions. Select dispositions that reinforce the identified skills. Prepare to help students understand the connection between the selected disposition and related skills.
    1.
    2.

Select and assign textual reading or other pre-discussion prepara-tion for students. Productive discussions spring from students thinking about issues as they access and use relevant knowledge. Regardless of the topic or content area, students need to prepare by delving into a related knowledge base. Typically, the teacher might assign students a text to read or a topic to research, perhaps using carefully selected online resources. The teacher might also have students respond to the proposed focus question in writing prior to the discussion. At other times, teachers might ask students to create questions related to the proposed topic of discussion—or questions related to the text on which the discussion will be based. To plan an appropriate pre-discussion assignment, teachers will need to consider the question or topic for discussion, students' ages and developmental levels, and the discipline or content area.

Pre-discussion Reading or Other Assignments

A. Reading From Text or Primary Sources. Text-based discussions support student focus on the question for discussion by providing a point of reference for their thinking and accountability for their points of view.

B. Independent Research on Topics Related to Discussion. Given student access to online information sources, independent research is a viable form of prereading and can yield a diversity of viewpoints. When this is the selected mode for student preparation, certain use-of-knowledge skills, such as "evaluates the credibility of information sources," become very critical.

C. Pre-Discussion Writing Assignment. Writing assignments assist students in clarifying their thinking as they prepare for a discussion.

D. Student Generation of Questions Related to a Discussion Topic. Students are more apt to pose questions during a discussion if they've had time to think about the topic in advance. A simple but powerful strategy is to preview the focus question the day before the discussion and invite students to generate true "wonderings" about the subject as a homework assignment.

Identify structures to activate and sustain thinking and to promote the participation of all students. As students hone their discussion skills, they need warm-ups to initiate their thinking—and time-outs to regroup if the momentum wanes or if they get off topic or lose focus. Teachers can anticipate these student needs by selecting thinking routines and protocols that "prime the pump" for productive discussion. For example, paired response strategies such as Think-Pair-Share and Turn and Talk can activate students' thinking as a discussion begins or jump-start a discussion that is floundering.

Sample Expectations for Participation in Online Discussions

1. Post your response to the focus question in complete sentences, providing a rationale or explanation for your ideas, including textual references.
2. Respond by the posted deadline date and time.
3. Read all of your classmates' postings.
4. Post a minimum of two responses to classmates' entries, including at least one question.

Online discussion forums are alternative vehicles for activating student thinking prior to a classroom discussion. Classroom management systems such as Edmodo, Schoology, and Moodle offer opportunities for threaded discussions that enable students to respond to an initial question and to one another. While some teachers choose to host a full-blown discussion using one of these tools, these online platforms can also be used to prime the pump before students enter a face-to-face discussion. When using one of these tools, you may wish to pose a question online that is somewhat different from the focus question for the in-class discussion. Remember the question related to Athenian democracy that was featured in Chapter 1? These social studies teachers might choose to pose this portion of the question online several days prior to the class discussion: *What were the relative benefits and disadvantages of Athenian democracy? Explain why you believe each identified feature to be either a benefit or disadvantage to Athenian society at large.*

Teachers might expect each student to post his or her own response to the focus question along with a minimum of two responses to classmates' ideas. This online discussion could prepare students to respond to the following in-class focus question: *In what ways would you suggest modifying Athenian democracy to make it workable in our community today?* The text box offers sample expectations for student participation in an online discussion. Additionally, teachers may wish to establish "netiquette," guidelines that usually include suggestions such as "no yelling" (i.e., using all caps or boldface). An online search will yield samples of such guidelines.

Selecting Structures and Strategies to Activate and Sustain Thinking and Speaking

A. Activation of Thinking

1. **Develop a prompt.** In a teacher-guided discussion, a prompt might invite students to engage in reflective writing before the discussion to establish focus and generate ideas or engage in dialogue with peers to focus their thinking and gain insights from others. Effective prompts help students see the relevance of the topic to their lives.

2. **Select a structure.** When activating thinking, use a response structure that will engage *all students* in responding to the prompt. Choose a structure from one of the three categories below, varying choice of structure over time.
   - **Online Platform.** Examples: Schoology, Edmodo, Moodle
   - **Paired Response.** Examples: Think-Pair-Share, Card Swap
   - **Small Group.** Examples: Synectics, People-Graph

B. Regaining Momentum or Focus, or Increasing Participation

1. **Anticipate problems** that might emerge in the discussion that could require a teacher intervention. Consider the following four situations, along with any others you can anticipate, given your students and the topic.
   - What if the class seems to be losing energy or enthusiasm, or if the discussion doesn't appear to be moving forward or going deeper?
   - What if students do not stay focused on the discussion question but continue to get off topic?

- What if students are not using text-based evidence—or use erroneous information—to support their positions?
- What if the majority of students are not speaking or participating?

2. **Possible interventions:**
   - Use paired response, such as Think-Pair-Share or Turn and Talk. (Have prepared prompts to use for this purpose.)
   - Refocus by posing a variation on the opening question, one prepared in connection with original thinking about the focus question.
   - Provide time-out for individual consolidation of thinking and writing, perhaps with the stipulation that each student thinks of a question he or she has about the conversation to this point.

Consider organizational issues. Prior to a given class discussion, the teacher must make a number of practical decisions, including the size of the discussion group and the arrangement of classroom furniture. Teacher-guided discussion can occur in at least three different student configurations: (1) whole-class, open forum in which all students are involved in a discussion and the teacher occupies the dual role of participant and (when appropriate) guide/facilitator; (2) fishbowl or inside-outside circles in which the teacher sits with some students in the inner circle and other students sit outside that circle with a listening assignment and the knowledge that they will rotate to the inner circle sometime during the class period; and (3) a small group of five to eight students facilitated by the teacher while other students work on a pre- or post-discussion activity or, perhaps, engage in a structured small-group discussion.

Discussion works best when participants can see one another. Hence, the optimal arrangement of desks or chairs is a circular or U-shaped formation. This can be a challenge for teachers who have overcrowded classrooms; who are not in the same classroom all day; or for those with multiple teaching assignments, which make it difficult to rearrange furniture for particular classes. Our best advice is to be creative and do the best you can, given the physical constraints. Some teachers move furniture to the edge of the room and have students sit on the floor in a circle. Others use the fishbowl, with a limited number of students (eight to ten) sitting in an inside circle and others outside with an active listening assignment. Students rotate in and out of the circle so that everyone has an opportunity to participate.

Organizational Considerations: Size, Configuration, and Floor Plan for Discussion Group

A. Size and Configuration
1. Whole class
2. Fishbowl *(Considerations: Number of students constituting each small discussion group, number of groups/rotations, and composition of groups)*
3. Teacher-facilitated small groups *(Considerations: Composition of each group, length of time for each small-group discussion, directions to be given to students when they are engaged in a pre- or post-discussion activity)*

B. Floor Plan
1. Large circle
2. Inside-outside circles
3. U-shaped arrangement
4. Other

The Template for Planning a Productive Discussion (see Appendix B) is the complete version of these segments. Individual teachers can use it to plan for upcoming discussions in their classrooms. Ideally, however, planning for discussion can become a collaborative endeavor, and colleagues who teach the same content can use the template to structure their work together. For teachers without access to a local planning partner, an option is to connect electronically with others who teach the same course or content by creating an online group for the planning of discussions.

Opening

The success of a discussion can depend on the "kick-off," which includes the following: ensuring that the players understand the "rules of the game" or the norms and guidelines for interacting one with another, focusing on the skills players need to be effective in their positions, providing the structures or line-ups to begin the play, and putting the question in play so that all are ready to receive it.

Review norms or guidelines. Chapter 1 emphasized the importance of norms or guidelines for classroom interactions. As the teacher, you can decide which "rules of the game" are appropriate for you and your students. We recommend that you consult the norms presented in Chapter 1 as you decide upon those most appropriate for your students. We suggest that you include norms from all three categories: purpose of questions, think times, and participation.

Focus on targeted skills and dispositions. In teacher-guided discussion, as in other forms of discussion, teachers set the stage for students to focus on particular discussion skills. An important outcome of the planning stage is the selection of a limited number of skills that are appropriate to the developmental level of students and to the requirements suggested by a particular topic or question for discussion. A highly effective model for presenting targeted discussion skills to students is presented in a Teaching Channel video that is accessible via the QR code on this page (Teaching Channel, 2015). In the video, Kelly Bouchard, a 4th grade teacher at Ellen P. Hubbell Elementary School in Bristol, Connecticut, engages her students in thinking about two discussion skills (framed as learning targets) that they practice in quads. Ms. Bouchard uses a small-group format to provide guided practice for her students. As she monitors the groups, she notes students' use of targeted skills, and her notes help her give students specific interim feedback. The salient features of this classroom example include a focus on a limited number of skills, engagement of students in defining the success criteria they will use to assess their progress in using these skills, and opportunities for guided practice with feedback.

Begin the play. Our experience suggests that more students become more engaged in discussion if the teacher strategically activates their thinking before the discussion begins. An activator or warm-up helps students focus on the topic at hand, collect their thoughts, and generate ideas. A host of structured activities might serve as activators. Here are three that we and teachers we've worked with have used successfully: Synectics, People-Graph, and Card Swap.

A *synectic* is a linguistic device that stimulates out-of-the box thinking. The word is a Greek derivative and means "the joining together of different ideas." A synectic activates students' thinking by asking them to compare two dissimilar ideas. For example:

As Mr. Brown prepares his 11th grade U.S. History students for a teacher-guided discussion on Roosevelt's decision to delay U.S. entry to World War II, he engages them in the following activity. First, he asks them to reflect silently and jot down individual responses to this question: *What is your view of isolationism?* After allowing several minutes for silent thinking and writing, Mr. Brown projects four images on the whiteboard: an island, a cocoon, a cave, and an oasis. He asks each student to choose the image that best represents his or her view of isolationism and to complete the following statement: *Isolationism is like [selected image] because* _____.

Mr. Brown points to four designated areas in the classroom for students to meet with others who selected the same image. The students form four groups, and each group selects a recorder to write its responses on chart paper. The chart paper for the students who selected "island" looks like this:

Isolationism is like <u>an island</u> because . . .

- You're protected from the turbulence that surrounds you.
- You can use resources to focus on your own needs.
- You become self-sufficient.
- It keeps you from getting involved in other people's business.
- You're afraid to venture too far from safe harbor.
- You might get stranded.

At the end of this activity, Mr. Brown presents the following focus question for discussion:

President Roosevelt delayed the United States' entry to World War II until after the Japanese attack on Pearl Harbor, at which time he declared war on Japan. He did not declare war on Germany until it joined its Axis ally in a declaration of war on the United States. Had you been a member of Roosevelt's cabinet, would you have supported or opposed his decision to pursue an isolationist policy for the first four years of World War II? Consider both the short- and long-term interests of the United States and the Allied powers as you offer support for your position.

When the question for discussion involves a debatable or controversial issue, teachers can use a People-Graph to engage all students in thinking about their position on the issue and sharing their thinking informally with a small group of peers before entering into a more formal discussion. This response strategy, like Synectics, begins with individual and silent reflection. The teacher prompts students to determine their level of agreement with a statement (e.g., from Strongly Disagree to Strongly Agree) and to jot down support for their position. After two to four minutes of silent rating and reflection, the teacher asks students to move to the spot on the People-Graph that corresponds to their position. Many teachers put tape on the floor at appropriate intervals—often from 10 (Strongly Agree) to 0 (Strongly Disagree)—to assist with the student line-up on the graph. When all students have "taken their stand" on the graph, the teacher invites them to gather with two or three peers who took a similar position and share their reasoning. The teacher might then "sample" students' various positions by hearing from two or three groups at different points on the line—or ask students to return to their seats to begin the formal discussion.

In the previous example, Mr. Brown could have used a People-Graph to activate student thinking and begin the discussion on Roosevelt's policy by asking them to consider the following statement: *Roosevelt's decision to delay U.S. entry into World War II until after the attack on Pearl Harbor was the best course of action.* Students would have been asked to take a position on the line from 0 (Strongly Disagree) to 10 (Strongly Agree).

If you were Mr. Brown, which strategy would you use—Synectics or People-Graph? Why?

The third activator of discussion—Card Swap (or Give-One/Get-One)—also begins with individual and silent reflection and writing in response to a prompt. In this case, students respond to a question on a note card, writing legibly with the foreknowledge that they will exchange cards with classmates who will then communicate their ideas to others. After an appropriate amount of time for a written response, students stand and find one other person with whom to share their thinking. Partners explain their responses to each other, and at the end of the exchange, they swap cards. Students then find another classmate with whom to share their first partner's ideas. Typically, students make three or four different exchanges during the five or six minutes allowed for the partner sharing and card exchange. This process primes the pump for discussion, as all students become engaged in thinking, talking, and listening to different perspectives in a fairly nonthreatening format. When the whole-class or larger group discussion begins, students have the benefit of their own thinking as well as that of others.

Think about how Mr. Brown might have used Card Swap to focus and generate student thinking about the Roosevelt decision. What question might he have used to prompt student thinking?

Online discussion is another strategy that can be used to stimulate student thinking about the topic for discussion prior to the actual kick-off of the discussion. Like the face-to-face activators, online conversations provide a structure for students to make personal connections with the discussion topic and with others' ideas before engaging in the discussion itself.

Present the question for discussion. Teachers will need to give forethought to the posing of the question to the class. We suggest that teachers think in terms of "presenting" a question, not "asking" it (Walsh & Sattes, 2005). Think of the difference. When we present something, we offer it as a gift of sorts to our audience. We are genuinely interested in the audience's reception; we demonstrate interest in their response. Presenting a quality focus question

Philosophical Chairs to Open a Discussion on Opposition to the Vietnam War

In this video lesson, Valerie Ziegler, an 11th grade U.S. history teacher at Abraham Lincoln High School in San Francisco, poses the following question to her students following their review of two primary source documents: *Why did people oppose the Vietnam War? Was it* mainly *for political, social, or economic reasons?* Using the Philosophical Chairs model, she directs each student to move physically to the section of the room designated for their point of view. She then guides the class in sharing the reasons for their selection and poses follow-up questions. Students refer to the text, build on one another's ideas, and listen actively to diverse points of view.

https://www.teachingchannel.org/videos/reading-like-a-historian-taking-positions

demonstrates real interest in students' responses. Such a presentation requires teachers to deliver the question in a way that shows they care about student responses—by using facial and vocal expressions and carefully chosen words. It means making eye contact with students to signal interest in them and their ideas (Walsh & Sattes, 2005). Projecting the focus question on a screen or writing it on a whiteboard keeps it in front of students for the duration of a session and allows the teacher to return student talk to the focus question by simply pointing to it.

The opening of a discussion sets the tone and often determines the level of student interest and engagement for the remainder of the discussion. Keys to an effective opening are the teacher's intentionality in focusing student attention on expected norms, targeted discussion skills and dispositions, and the focus question itself. An effective kick-off, however, does not ensure a game-winning performance. For that to happen, the teacher must support the continued thinking and participation of students by "sustaining the play."

Sustaining

A productive discussion ensues when participants maintain focus on the question at issue, speak and listen to one another, consider one another's perspectives as they extend their individual and collective thinking, and pose questions to clarify or extend others' thinking or to share questions. These participant behaviors serve to keep a discussion alive and moving; they form the heart and soul of a discussion. As teachers guide a discussion, one of their primary roles is to make strategic moves that elicit and support these student behaviors (i.e., by modeling, scaffolding, and coaching).

Teachers face a number of challenges in sustaining a discussion, such as (1) helping students become comfortable with and honor silence, (2) extending individual student thinking and speaking, (3) encouraging students to build on one another's thinking instead of simply promoting their own perspectives, (4) keeping students on topic and "reeling in" students who seem intent on hijacking the discussion and taking it in a completely different direction, (5) jump-starting a stalled discussion, (6) nurturing curiosity and excitement, and (7) ensuring equitable participation—encouraging reticent or shy students and managing would-be monopolizers.

A key to sustaining a discussion and addressing these challenges is the teacher's skillful use of the questioning strategies introduced in Chapter 1—framing a question for discussion (including follow-up questions), promoting equitable participation, scaffolding student thinking, and creating a thoughtful and respectful culture. Brookfield and Preskill (2005) suggest that the skills of questioning, listening, and responding are "at the heart of sustaining an engaging discussion" and that "of the three, learning to question takes the most skill and practice" (p. 85). We suggest that teachers focus on three things as they plan for and guide this stage of discussion: (1) listen to understand; (2) scaffold with statements, questions, or other appropriate moves; and (3) monitor to ensure equitable participation.

Listen to understand. One of the most important norms for quality questioning is the intentional use of two types of pauses, called "wait times" or "think times" (introduced in Chapter 1). The first think time is the pause after a teacher or student asks a question. This silence allows time for everyone to consider what they know about the question. The second think time—the silence after a participant stops speaking but before another intervenes—gives the speaker time to extend or modify his or her comments and gives listeners time to process the speaker's comments. When teachers work with students to create a culture in which think times are consistently honored, everyone (including the teacher) has an opportunity to listen to understand. Honoring and using think time helps students develop the following listening skills:

- Using silence after a classmate stops speaking to think about what he or she said and to compare the speaker's thinking to one's own.
- Asking questions to better understand the speaker's point of view.
- Waiting before adding one's own ideas to ensure that the speaker has completed his or her thoughts.
- Accurately paraphrasing what another student says.
- Looking at the speaking student and giving nonverbal cues that one is paying attention.

During a teacher-guided discussion, teachers can model each of these skills for students, and they can be explicit in doing so. How? By focusing on the student who is speaking. By looking at the speaker and nodding or using other nonverbal signals to convey full attention. By being "in the moment" and focusing on the speaker's words rather than on one's own views. These require the habits of mind described earlier in this chapter: appreciative listening, valuing student contributions, focused thinking, and fair-mindedness. Acquiring these habits demands discipline and practice.

This type of listening also requires teachers to take off their evaluator hats and refrain from giving immediate corrective feedback or praise, either of which can break the flow of student thought and conversation. A teacher's goal when guiding a discussion is to move from "*evaluator* of student thinking to *sustainer* of student thinking" (Juzwik et al., 2013, p. 30). This is a difficult transition for most of us, as we often listen for gaps in students' understanding so we can offer instant formative feedback. Giving up this expert role, however, is one of the keys to sustaining discussion. Doing so requires teachers to engage with students in their thinking.

When we are able to be in the moment with a student, we can use the silence after he or she stops speaking to think about the meaning of his or her words and to allow another student to respond. Should there be no response after a reasonable wait—perhaps up to 10 seconds—we can pose a question to get behind the speaker's thinking, invite the speaker to extend his or her thoughts, or paraphrase the student's comments, checking to ensure that we have interpreted them correctly. Following the paraphrase, we might invite other students to agree or disagree with a rationale, reminding them that a primary listening skill is to use the silence following someone's comments to compare what he or she said to what they (as listeners) were thinking.

Listening to understand helps address a number of the challenges associated with sustaining a productive discussion. When a teacher models being comfortable with silence—and comments on its value—this communicates and reinforces the purpose and value of silence. Silences can encourage students to build on one another's ideas rather than simply advocate for their own. Many students require assistance in using silence to build a discussion, and teachers can scaffold this skill in a number of ways. As mentioned earlier, a simple strategy is to paraphrase what a student says and invite other students to agree or disagree or to piggyback on or extend the speaker's comment. If this fails to yield a reaction from another student, the teacher might model the behavior of "asking questions to understand the speaker's point of view." Imagine a classroom in which the teacher makes all of these moves in a very purposeful manner. To ensure that students can identify the skills being modeled—and how those skills contribute to discussion—this teacher might, when the time is right, put the discussion temporarily on hold and reflect aloud, saying something like this:

> I want to step back and share with you how I was attempting to use a number of our listening skills. First, I waited after John stopped speaking to be sure he had finished expressing his thoughts and had nothing else to add. I also used the silence to think about what he was saying. I tried to set aside my ideas about the topic and focus on John's ideas.

I was waiting to allow one of you to make a comment or pose a question to John—because the purpose of discussion is for you to talk to one another, not just to me. When no one spoke, I paraphrased what I understood John to mean, to be certain that I really understood his intended meaning, and I invited him to confirm my understanding and to extend his thinking if he desired. Again, my hope was that one of you would respond to John after he nodded in agreement with my restatement of his ideas.

Because I had a question about one of John's statements, I was ready to pose a question to him if no one else spoke. However, I believe that each of you can either agree or disagree with one of John's ideas. So I want us to return to our conversation, allowing some silence for each of us to identify one of John's main ideas and decide what we think about his position and why we think as we do—or decide if we have a question that was sparked by John's comments.

Modeling has minimal effect without this type of teacher reflection. Not all students will pick up on what we are attempting to teach through example alone.

This kind of explicit teacher reflection helps ensure that intentional modeling results in student learning. Of course, it is important to take care that we do not interrupt the flow of a discussion with such an intervention. When students are speaking to one another without our prompting, the teacher's think-aloud would be neither necessary nor productive. However, when a discussion reaches a standstill (which they sometimes do), such interventions can serve two purposes: (1) they can provide direct instruction about discussion skills and processes, and (2) they can jump-start the discussion, especially when the teacher ends the think-aloud by inviting students to continue the conversation. In fact, this type of reflection is an example of a scaffold, which is the second important focus area for teacher thinking during a discussion.

Scaffold with questions, statements, or other appropriate moves. In this section, we look back to a number of the common challenges teachers confront in discussions and consider alternative ways they can scaffold individual and group thinking and speaking to overcome these challenges. Figure 3.2 lists

Figure 3.2 | **Scaffolds Associated with Five Challenges Related to Sustaining Teacher-Guided Discussion**

Challenge	Teacher Statements	Teacher Questions	Structures	Student Questions
Extending individual student thinking and speaking	• Statements of interest • Phatics • Fillers • Paraphrases and reflective statements • Declarative statements • Statements of mind	• Uptake questions • Metacognitive questions	• Signals/non-verbals	• Teacher invitation for student questions
Guiding students to self-assess and self-correct	• Paraphrases and reflective statements • Statements of mind	• Metacognitive questions		• Teacher invitation for student questions
Encouraging students to build on one another's thinking	• Speaker connection • Revoicing	• Inviting a student to piggyback on a classmate's statement		• Teacher invitation for student questions
Keeping students on topic	• Declarative statements	• Metacognitive questions • Call attention to focus question	• Parking lot	
Jump-starting a stalled discussion	• Statement of teacher view	• "True" questions or wonderings • Follow-up question to original focus question	• Think-Pair-Share • Write-Pair-Share • Other structured or paired protocols	
Nurturing student curiosity and excitement	• Statement of teacher view	• "True" questions or wonderings		• Encouraging and scaffolding student questions

five of these challenges and scaffolds that can be employed to address each. We describe the various scaffolds with the challenges to which they relate.

Extending individual student thinking and speaking. One distinguishing feature of discussion, as compared to recitation or more usual classroom talk, is that students speak at length. Through such extended speaking, they clarify and sometimes correct their own thinking. However, students who have little experience in discussion are unlikely to engage in such exploratory, tentative, and reflective thinking. Teachers can support this through use of a variety of scaffolds, which serve different purposes.

When the purpose is to encourage students to continue talking, teachers can make a short statement of interest in what the student is saying. Examples include, "That's a novel idea. I'd like to hear more," or simply, "You seem to be on to something here. I'm intrigued as to what prompted this idea." Alternatively, teachers can use what Dillon (1994) refers to as *phatics*—brief phrases that encourage a speaker to continue. For example, imagine that a student is explaining how he or she solved a word problem and stops speaking before addressing all steps. The teacher might make a short statement such as "We're with you," "Keep going," or "This is interesting." Such statements "have substantial effects on discussion . . . [enhancing] the length and initiative of children's responses far more than questions did, whether open or closed questions" (Dillon, 1994, p. 88). Another strategy, which most of us have used, is what Dillon calls *fillers*—words or sounds that convey you are listening to a student. Examples include "mm-hmm," "uh-huh," "mm," "I see," "I understand," and "OK." Finally, nonverbals—maintaining eye contact, nodding your head, and making various hand signals—can serve to encourage continued speaking.

Teachers can also extend student thinking by offering deeper comments. The paraphrasing of a student's comment followed by a personal reflection is a way of inviting the student to continue talking without posing an actual question. For example, after restating your understanding of a student's statement, you might simply say, "I hadn't thought of the issue in this manner, but I'm interested in hearing more about your reasoning." Similarly, you can offer a statement that conveys how you are thinking or feeling about a student's comment without restating it. In response to the comment of a student who offers real out-of-the-box thinking, you might comment, "I've not encountered this interpretation. I'm curious as to how you might explain this to an expert in this field." These types of teacher comments should be offered only after an extended pause that affords students the opportunity to respond to the speaker. A rule of thumb is to never preempt a student during discussion.

You may be wondering whether questions are ever an appropriate means of requesting continued thinking and speaking. Consider *uptake questions,* which incorporate some element of a student's idea or previous response in a request for further elaboration (Juzwik et al., 2013). Uptake questions might sound like this: "You are disagreeing with the author's point of view. How would you explain her point of view?" or "You told us you think Goldilocks should not have gone into the Bears' home. Can you say more about why you think this was a poor choice?" Researchers have found that the use of uptake questions correlates with student literacy and content learning. They "shift responsibility for thinking back to students . . . encourage student elaborations, and increase student thinking and engagement" (Michener & Ford-Connors, 2013, p. 91). They are also "key indicators of classrooms where student ideas shape learning" (Boyd & Galda, 2011, p. 96).

Guiding students to self-assess and self-correct. These scaffolds serve to invite students to continue on a given course of thinking. Often, however, a teacher wants students to reflect on, clarify, and perhaps even correct their thinking. When this is the case, the first impulse is usually to question. However, overuse of questions for this purpose can derail a discussion by signaling that the teacher is returning to the expert role. Again, statements or comments are less intrusive and are less likely to cause students to "freeze up," fearing they are wrong. Consider the value of the following kinds of statements in lieu of questions when the purpose is to get behind or even challenge student thinking: paraphrases, declarative statements, and statements of mind.

By paraphrasing, or restating what a student has said in our own words, we test our understanding of the meaning behind a comment. The student can either affirm our understanding and elaborate, or clarify his or her intended meaning. Similarly, we can simply repeat a portion of a student's comments, essentially reflecting them back to the speaker for reaction. Both of these strategies rebroadcast the speaker's thinking, which can encourage continued speaking.

Declarative statements are statements of fact that a teacher can use to call a student's attention to a factual error. For example, suppose a student comments, "Forest fires are terrible things. They destroy plant and animal life." The teacher's first impulse might be to ask, "Are there any benefits that result from forest fires?" Such a question might turn this discussion into a recitation. An alternative would be to make a statement such as, "Forest fires do destroy plant and animal life. They also regenerate forests by allowing for the development of new life." This statement would allow the speaker or other students to either continue the conversation or ask a question about the teacher's statement. Declarative statements can be very helpful in scaffolding use-of-knowledge skills, including accuracy and the referencing of texts or other information sources.

Statements of mind convey a teacher's reaction to a student remark or observation and can embody a question about the student's thinking. Examples include "I'm not following your line of reasoning," "I'm wondering what evidence you have for this assertion," and "I am a bit confused by . . ." This type of statement can be used to scaffold use-of-knowledge skills in a discussion (e.g., accuracy and citation of textual evidence) as well as cognitive skills (e.g., revealing assumptions and seeking clarification in an indirect manner).

Though we recommend that a teacher's first recourse in scaffolding an individual student's thinking and speaking be through making statements, questions are at times the more appropriate course. When a student's thinking seems muddled or is not transparent, metacognitive questions can help a student work through his or her thinking. These questions "call the learners' attention to their own thinking and use of knowledge," thereby enabling them to self-assess, self-correct, and build new understandings (Cazden, 2001, p. 92). Eleanor Duckworth (as cited in Cazden) elaborates on teacher questions that assist students and assess their learning:

> To the extent that one carries on a conversation with a child as a way of trying to understand a child's understanding, the child's understanding increases "in the very process." The questions that the interlocutor asks in an attempt to clarify for him/herself what the child is thinking oblige the child to think a little further also. . . . What do you mean? How did you do that? Why do you say that? How does that fit with what was just said? I don't really get that: could you explain it another way? Could you give me an example? How did you figure it out? In every case, those questions are primarily a way for the interlocutor to try to understand what the other is understanding. Yet in every case, also, they engage the other's thoughts and take them a step further. (Cazden, 2001, p. 92)

Taking student thinking a step further is precisely what scaffolding seeks to accomplish. The questions included in the Duckworth statement suggest the importance of getting behind student thinking and revealing the knowledge base and assumptions on which it is based. This is an important function for teachers as they guide discussions. Teacher questions that help students think about what they think and know can engage them in metacognitive thinking and model how they can use these types of questions to move their own and their classmates' understanding forward.

Encouraging students to build on one another's thinking. The skills we associate with collaboration enable students to move beyond a discussion that looks like ping-pong to one that is more akin to soccer. Most students have had limited practice in using these skills in school. Teacher scaffolds can nurture and support student interaction and collaboration. We offer three strategies that can serve this purpose: speaker connection, revoicing, and speaker invitation.

One relatively simple strategy is a speaker connection, a comment by the teacher connecting what one student says to the ideas of a previous student. This encourages dialogue between the two students and demonstrates two important collaborative and cognitive skills: piggybacking and connection making. Teachers can use this technique to model for students the value of listening to one another and building on others' ideas. This can accustom students to talking to one another and collaboratively seeking new understandings, rather than responding unilaterally and talking to the teacher. A speaker connection might start like this: "Maria, your comment connects to what Josh said earlier," with the teacher explicitly pointing out a specific connection between Maria's comment and Josh's.

Another type of teacher scaffold that encourages students to talk to and build on one another's ideas is *revoicing*, in which the teacher makes a statement that incorporates some aspect of a student's comment or idea. For example, during a class discussion on Newton's First Law of Motion, a student says, "Well, a basket of apples has more mass than just one apple, so it takes more force to move the basket than it takes to move a single apple." The teacher revoices by saying, "Susan said it takes more force to move an object with greater mass, in this case more force to move a basket of apples than a single apple. I'm wondering what this tells us about the relationship between mass and force." In this case, revoicing serves two purposes: it uses a student's insight to maintain an important content thread, and it also invites other students to build on this insight. In Cazden's (2001) view, "revoicing can be one strategy for building both an ever-increasing stock of common knowledge and an ever-increasing community of learners" (p. 91).

Teachers also scaffold student interaction by directly inviting students to ask questions of one another—and by making time for students to formulate and pose questions (another productive use of silence/think time!). A teacher invitation might take the form of a statement such as "Abby has offered one interpretation of this character's motive. I'm wondering if Abby's comments raise questions for anyone else about what makes this character tick."

Keeping students on topic. Many teachers are reticent to open the doors to true discussion because of past experiences with students wandering far afield from the focus question during the discussion. Keeping students on topic presents a special challenge because we never want to be so rigid that we squelch creative, out-of-the-box thinking, but our job is to ensure that discussions promote intended academic purposes and that students discipline their thinking in pursuit of a shared point of inquiry. Some of the preceding strategies can be used to this end. For example, a teacher might make a simple declarative statement such as "John, your comment is interesting, but it doesn't appear relevant to this topic for discussion. Could you write this on a sticky note and put it on our parking lot?" Likewise, the teacher might pose a metacognitive question such as "In what way does your comment relate to today's topic for discussion?" We recommend posting the focus question and the purpose for discussion in a prominent space in the classroom so that it's easy to employ the simple nonverbal gesture of pointing to the question in order to cue students that they need to refocus.

Jump-starting a stalled discussion. Another fear that some teachers have is that student talk will fizzle out before true exploration of the topic has begun or before deepening of understanding has occurred. What is a teacher to do in this case? The most accessible move is to provide the opportunity for partner talk. This can be as simple as asking students to turn and talk to an "elbow partner" to generate a question or comment that might move the discussion forward. A similar strategy that is often more productive is Write-Pair-Share: students take one or two minutes for silent, individual thinking and writing, then exchange views with a partner. Using structures such as these can scaffold participation by all.

Taking time for individual reflection and pair talk might not fit into your conception of scaffolding. Teachers are most familiar with scaffolding in the context of directly helping students reach a curricular standard, often during a class recitation, to build a bridge from where a student is to the desired level of knowledge or skill embodied in a standard. In the context of discussion, however, scaffolding is used to deepen students' content knowledge *and* develop their discussion skills. These things won't happen if students don't participate in the discussion—and in order to participate, they must feel confident that they have something worth saying. The use of pair talk can provide that confidence.

Pair talk is an example of peer scaffolding, which is sometimes more helpful to students than scaffolding offered by the teacher. Consider this definition of *scaffolding*:

> *Scaffolding* is the help given to a learner that is tailored to that learner's needs in achieving his or her goals of the moment. The best scaffolding provides this help in a way that contributes to learning. For example, telling someone how to do something or doing it for them may help them accomplish their immediate goal; but it is not scaffolding because the child does not actively participate in the construction of knowledge. In contrast, effective scaffolding provides prompts and hints that help learners figure it out on their own. (Sawyer, 2009, p. 11)

This definition allows for a range of scaffolds, including but not limited to teacher questions or comments. In any event, it is the teacher who must plan and allow time for all types of scaffolds.

Another teacher move that can serve as a catalyst to renew student participation is a statement of a personal view. When a discussion stalls, the teacher might convey his or her thinking about the issue at hand, offering it as just one of many possibilities. In doing so, the teacher enters the discussion as a full-fledged participant. It is best to refrain from using this tactic unless the discussion seems to be reaching a lull or stalemate. This teacher move carries with it the risk of shutting down student thinking because many students hesitate to disagree with the teacher.

A final strategy for breathing new life into a discussion is to pose a new question, one that addresses the topic or issue for discussion but comes at it from a slightly different angle. In Chapter 1, we suggested that teachers anticipate different directions student thinking might take in response to a focus question and prepare follow-up questions to scaffold when talk does not proceed as planned or hoped for. Having related questions in one's hip pocket can be good insurance against having a discussion come to a complete halt.

Nurturing student curiosity and excitement. Student curiosity and authentic interest in a topic fuel productive discussions. Without these, discussions really never get off the ground; talk is ho-hum, and students are disengaged and bored. How, then, do teachers support or scaffold curiosity and excitement? Besides framing a question that is worthy of collaborative investigation, perhaps the most important teacher behavior is to model curiosity and excitement by asking true questions and encouraging student questions. Teachers nurture student curiosity by asking questions when teachers themselves convey out loud their own perplexities or wonderings. When teachers pose "true" questions (that is, questions for which they do not have an answer or a preconceived point of view), they can stimulate student curiosity and extend thinking. During teacher-guided discussions, this type of question serves as a model for student inquiry.

Ultimately, student questions are the most important contributors to maintaining a discussion and excitement about the inquiry. Unfortunately, as we've previously stated, student questions are rare in most classrooms. While student questions can be scaffolds for sustaining thinking and discussion, teachers often need to scaffold students' willingness and ability to ask questions. This begins with communicating to students the reasons why they might pose questions to one another (and to themselves) about a text or topic. Figure 3.3 is a useful tool for scaffolding students' development of the six question-asking skills discussed in Chapter 2.

Figure 3.3 | **Prompts and Stems to Scaffold Students'
Development of Question-Asking Skills**

Skill	Use When	Sample Stems/Standard Questions
Poses questions to clarify and better understand the substance of a topic or text	• You are confused by terminology, wording, or sentence structure. • You need additional information.	• What did the author mean when she wrote …? • What do you mean when you say …? • Can you say that in a different way? • Can you provide an example?
Asks questions to identify a speaker's assumption	• You do not understand what is behind a speaker's (or author's) thinking. • You think the speaker might be basing an argument on emotions, not facts.	• I'm wondering if you have personal beliefs that influence your thinking about this. • What experiences have you had that cause you to believe _____?
Poses questions to clarify the thinking or reasoning behind an argument or conclusion	• You do not follow a line of thinking or reasoning; that is, you don't know how a speaker got from A to B. • You think a speaker might be overgeneralizing.	• I hadn't thought of it in this way. Can you tell me what led you to this conclusion? • Would this always be true? What might change the outcome?
Surfaces and questions own assumptions	• You genuinely wonder whether a personal belief is affecting your perspective. • You realize that the evidence is counter to what you first thought about a topic.	• How are my personal beliefs affecting my openness to others? • What contributed to my beliefs? • Am I willing to listen to these facts even though they are contradictory to my beliefs?
Asks questions when curious	• You have a "true" wondering about something; you have a question for which you don't have an answer.	• How can we find out more information? • What effect would that have? • What might have caused this?
Asks "what if" questions to encourage divergent thinking	• You want to encourage the speaker to consider a different point of view. • You have an idea that you want to test with the group.	• What might be an alternative way of thinking? • What if …? • Imagine _____. How might this affect our thinking?

A final word about questions as scaffolds. You may have been surprised at our admonition to consider alternative scaffolds before defaulting to questions—especially in view of the fact that this book focuses on questioning for discussion! Our focus is on *quality questioning practices*—not just prompts ending with question marks.

We are aware that many associate—and sometimes even equate—questions with scaffolding. Based upon his research, J. T. Dillon (1994) argued against the use of teacher questions in discussion, suggesting they "will foil discussion processes, turning the class into some other group talk much like recitation." He further stated that, during a discussion, "teacher questions do not stimulate student thinking and they do not encourage participation. They depress student thought and talk" (p. 78). We agree with Dillon that questions, when used to interrogate students, can stifle their speaking, but we believe teacher questions do have a role in teacher-guided discussions.

While teacher questions can scaffold student thinking in discussion, there are a number of caveats. First, teachers need to pay special attention to their affect and nonverbal signals as they pose questions. Think back to the teacher dispositions highlighted earlier in this chapter, particularly appreciative listening. If a teacher's facial expression and body language convey that he or she is intently listening to truly understand the meaning behind a student's words, then the student is likely to receive the question as an expression of true interest in what he is thinking. And if the teacher's language conveys a valuing of the student contribution, the student may interpret the question as a genuine effort to help clarify or support his thinking. This type of questioning is unlikely to derail the discussion or turn it into a recitation; rather, it can serve as a model for students to use as they interact with one another.

Second, the wording of our questions can convey a true interest in hearing the student say more about a topic—either to clarify or extend thinking—rather than evaluating or scrutinizing student comments. Some useful lead-ins to questions are "I have a wondering," "I'm curious about . . . ," and "Your comment raises a question for me." These prefaces to questions, when delivered with genuine interest, convey respect and offer students a comfortable, safe space for responding.

Third, it is important to consider ways to engage the entire class in thinking about the question we pose rather than setting up a one-on-one conversation with a single student. A potential downside of teacher questioning during discussion is that nonresponding students may default to passive positions, considering the conversation to be only between the teacher and the speaker. Teachers can identify a point of personal confusion or interest and then invite other students to ask a question that might clarify the speaker's position.

Fourth, as previously emphasized, we need to be certain that the question we have in mind is a better device than a statement to prompt further student thinking and speaking. Remember, during teacher-guided discussion, the purpose is to model for students the skills, behaviors, and dispositions needed for independent discussions, within and beyond the classroom. The teacher should set the expectation for students to talk to one another and to build on one another's ideas, not to interrogate and constantly challenge one another.

In the end, the choice of which move to make—offering a statement, asking a question, deferring talk to other students, or extending silence—should depend on which move is most likely to sustain student thought and talk at a given point in the discussion. This is a judgment that teachers can make only in the moment of a class discussion. McCann (2014, p. 124) summarizes a number of dialogic moves that mirror the ones we highlighted:

- Connecting student comments in a discussion to previous class activities, including small-group work and long- and short-term learning targets.
- Soliciting responses and paraphrasing to affirm students, without endorsing "right answers."
- Inviting students to assess or evaluate one another's contributions.
- Monitoring the development of student thinking to determine the appropriate timing for a teacher to intervene with a statement or question.
- Summarizing the thread of a discussion and identifying possible areas for deeper talk.

Scaffolding student thinking and speaking is one of the most rigorous tasks in teaching; it requires focused listening, thinking, and real-time formulation of appropriate prompts. This is one reason we suggest that teachers anticipate possible student responses as they frame the focus question during the planning stage. Although scaffolding is usually considered to be a support for student use of cognitive and use-of-knowledge skills, it can also be used to support equity in discussions—if teachers are aware of who is speaking, or not, and how much.

Monitor to ensure equitable participation. Equitable participation is a hallmark of democratic discussion, and it does not happen automatically.

Bridges (1979) states that "discussion requires that each participant will be allowed to hear and be heard and, beyond this, presupposes at least some degree of equality" with regard to individual group members' expressions of opinions and interests (p. 23). He suggests that when teachers are unable to shed the expert/evaluator role, many students are reticent to express what they think. It is not enough that teachers shed this expert role, however. They must also proactively monitor participation if they are to ensure that all voices are heard. This is one of the most daunting challenges teachers face as they facilitate and guide student discussion.

Track patterns of participation. One goal for a collaborative discussion is the participation of all students. The challenges of restraining would-be monopolizers and encouraging nonparticipants are relevant to this goal. Addressing these challenges during teacher-guided discussions requires that teachers find a way to keep track of which students are speaking, and how much. The teacher can assume this responsibility or ask a student to help. Either way, the teacher needs to maintain an ongoing awareness of patterns of participation. The monitoring

Content-Specific Considerations in the Mathematics Classroom

Discussion in a mathematics classroom involves no less scaffolding and connection making than discussion in other disciplines. The context for discussion, however, is different in that it most usually revolves around deepening understanding of mathematical concepts by focusing on student responses to a math question or problem that is cognitively challenging. Teachers make student thinking visible by posing questions that "probe and explore meaning and relationships [pressing] students to explain the why of their thinking" (Smith & Stein, 2011, p. 73). In 5 *Practices for Orchestrating Productive Mathematics Discussion*, Smith and Stein argue that teachers, when guiding a discussion, need to create a balance between student *authorship* (constructing their own mathematical understandings) and student *accountability* for developing understandings central to the discipline of mathematics. This book provides a useful framework for organizing discussions in mathematics classrooms.

piece is relatively simple; the greater challenge is how to ensure that all students have a voice in the class conversation.

Be proactive. One strategy is to be proactive by working with students to establish participation norms for discussion. (See Chapter 1 for examples.) Posting agreed-upon norms can support equitable participation. For instance, a teacher who observes one student beginning to monopolize a discussion can point to the following norm: *Monitor your talk so as not to monopolize.* Alternatively, the teacher might ask for a time-out from the discussion and say, "I'm observing that only a few of you are participating in our discussion today. I want to remind us of two of our participation norms: *Share what you are thinking so others can learn from you* and *Encourage others to speak, particularly those who are not participating.* [Points to norms and pauses.] Think about your own and others' contributions to our conversation so far. [Pauses again.] Now reflect on what you can do to be sure everyone participates."

Beyond the teaching and posting of participation norms, there are at least three other ways teachers can support student participation:

Use think time 2. Asking students to wait for at least three to five seconds following a peer's comment gives all students time to process what the speaker has said and to think about their reactions. Many students require this processing time. The thinking of "internal processors" can be shut down by students who have a response out of their mouths before the speaker finishes. When all students have time to process and think, they are more likely to have something to contribute and will have greater confidence to speak. Think time 2 can potentially curb the talk of monopolizers by encouraging them to think before blurting out the first thing that comes to their minds. Using think time to encourage student participation requires that students understand and practice the think time norms presented in Chapter 1.

Try Think-Pair-Share. Another strategy to promote equitable participation is to take a brief time-out, call for individual reflection, and follow up with paired responses. This strategy is useful not only for scaffolding continued thinking when a discussion begins to fizzle (as mentioned earlier) but also for leveling the playing field. Each student responds in writing, by speaking to a partner, or both. After partner talk, the teacher can call on a student who has not spoken to share something discussed with a partner.

Use direct invitations as appropriate. Sometimes it is appropriate to request comments from students who have not yet contributed. The teacher can either issue an open invitation to all nonparticipants or call on a student by name. All teachers recognize the downside of spotlighting individual students who are not contributing—for example, they risk embarrassing the student or inviting an inappropriate remark. Teachers also know how to read students' nonverbal cues. Sometimes students are waiting to speak but can't find an opening because more aggressive classmates are dominating. We can honor these students by simply stating, "I sense that ___ has something to add," and pausing to allow the student to speak (or not).

Text Talk Time in a 5th Grade ELA Classroom

In this videotaped lesson, 5th grade teacher Stacy Brewer engages her students in discussion to prepare them for an individual writing assignment. Prior to entering the discussion circle, students engaged in small-group brainstorming (opening activity). Ms. Brewer sits in a circle with the students as she facilitates their discussion. She begins by reviewing guidelines and expectations with students, which include speaking one at a time, listening carefully to peers, and using hand signals to indicate a desire to speak (two fingers up if they want to add to what someone else said and a thumb up if they want to add something new). Ms. Brewer sustains the discussion by listening carefully to each speaker, asking follow-up questions, sometimes making a textual reference herself, and seeking to ensure participation by a wide range of students. She is explicit with students about what she is doing as she leads them in this discussion. She uses both whole-group discussion and think-pair-share during this seven-minute video.

https://www.teachingchannel.org/videos/analyzing-text-as-a-group

Set realistic growth targets for yourself. Sustaining discussions demands a great deal of teachers: laserlike focus, extraordinary listening, quick thinking, restraint and diplomacy, sensitivity to individual students, deep knowledge of the content or discipline, good judgment, and more. These are skills that teachers develop and refine over time. It is always possible to get better at sustaining discussions, but teachers shouldn't try to do everything at once. Just as teachers help students develop a few discussion skills at a time, they will need to concentrate on a limited number of behaviors related to sustaining student discussion during any given lesson. We recommend that teachers develop growth targets for themselves so that they can focus their efforts and reflect on their performance.

Closing

What is the most appropriate way to close a discussion? In part, this depends on the question for discussion and the related purpose. Most academic discussions are intended to provide students with opportunities to deepen or extend their understanding or perspective. Although the theory behind discussion is that collaborative thinking and talking can promote this end, it is at the individual student level that understanding is deepened or extended. Each student will derive something different from every discussion, depending on at least three factors: (1) depth and breadth of background and disciplinary knowledge, (2) beliefs and values born of individual experiences, and (3) proficiency in skills associated with discussion. Because students have different "starting points," they will learn and grow in different ways through the practice of discussion. Hence, the closings for discussions provide opportunities for individual students to reflect on and consolidate their thinking. They do not require that the class as a whole reach closure on the discussion topic.

Assist students in consolidating their thinking. Nystrand and his colleagues (1997) argue that learning through discussion occurs as a teacher and students talk together to "compose shared understandings that in turn contribute to individual students' learning" and that student learning "emerges from the interplay of voices" (p. ix). They also distinguish between students as "producers of information" during discussions and students as "reproducers of information" in most traditional classroom interactions (p. 80). Additionally, they make a distinction between individual student learning and collective or shared learning. Each student becomes a producer of his or her own learning as well as a contributor to shared understandings.

The closing or termination of talk about the substance of a discussion, then, is the time for students to assimilate their own and others' thinking into their individual mental frameworks and schema. At this point, most students can benefit from teacher assistance in the form of coaching, particularly if they are just starting their apprenticeship. One coaching strategy a teacher can use is to pose questions to the whole class as a discussion comes to a close. The following is a possible sequence of questions:

- What was the key issue in question throughout our discussion?
- What different perspectives, points of view, or directions in thinking emerged?
- What evidence was offered in support of each of these?
- What inferences can we make from the evidence offered?
- What are the lingering questions?
- What additional questions can we generate?

The teacher might chart responses to these questions (or ask a student to do so). Following whole-class thinking and talking about these questions, the teacher can allow time for individual student reflection and journaling. The closing can occur during the same class period as the discussion or the next day.

An alternative approach is to begin with individual reflective writing and have students share their insights with the rest of the class. One way to structure student reflection is to use the "I Used to Think/Now I Think/I Still Wonder" prompt and ask students to record their reflections in a three-column format.

Help discussants identify emerging or unanswered questions. Both of these strategies are likely to generate additional questions. We believe that most good discussions lead to student generation of additional questions. Teachers will need to resist the temptation to reach definitive closure and tie a ribbon around a student conversation. The important thing is to provide time for students to engage in individual reflection and processing so they can organize any new learning into their minds and ponder residual or emerging questions.

Reflecting

The final stage of the discussion cycle is reflection on the process of discussion, which can occur in two venues: (1) in the classroom, where the teacher reflects with students and guides them in collaborative reflection; and (2) outside the classroom, where the teacher reflects alone and, ideally, with other colleagues. Call to mind a post-game analysis during which the coach and players reflect on how players performed while on the field of play, and the coaching staff evaluates the game plan itself.

We imagine two possible types of in-class reflection: individual reflective writing by students, in response either to survey items or to open-ended prompts, and a collective reflective dialogue or debrief facilitated by the teacher. Individual reflection can feed into class reflection when teachers provide opportunities for both kinds of after-action thinking. However, depending on purpose and available time, a teacher may decide to engage students in only one of these modes of reflection.

Facilitate individual student reflection and self-assessment. Individual reflections focus on the discussion skills and dispositions the teacher selected during the planning stage and presented to students during the opening. These skills might have been identified as learning targets during the opening. Figure 3.4 presents a template teachers can use to solicit students' written responses regarding their own and classmates' use of targeted skills. Teachers ask students to write the skill areas—social, cognitive, and use of knowledge—that were the focus for their discussion in the left column. Because discussion is a collaborative process, students should be asked to reflect on their individual performances as well as their class's collective performance: *In what ways did they as individuals seek to use identified skills and dispositions? To what extent did all students in the class collaborate to create the kind of conversation expected?* The ideal time for students to reflect on their performance is immediately after the discussion. If this is not possible, students might be asked to reflect on their performance as a homework assignment or during the next class period.

In the Teaching Channel video mentioned earlier (2015), 4th grade teacher Kelly Bouchard checked in with her students after they engaged in the first of two parts of a collaborative discussion on *Tuck Everlasting.* She first reminded them

Figure 3.4 | **Written Assessment of Targeted Discussion Skills**

Record each of the skill areas we focused on today in the first column. Then rate your use of this skill today, from VS (very skillful) to OK (acceptable) to NW (needs work), and give an example of why you rated yourself the way you did. Finally, rate your group's use of this skill, and provide an example.

Skill Area Focus	My Performance	Class or Group Performance
Contribute equitably to the discussion.	(VS) —— OK —— NW I spoke, but not too much. I think I made a good point.	VS —— (OK) —— NW Not everyone spoke until we asked one what she thought.
Ask questions to clarify what others say.	VS —— (OK) —— NW I didn't need to clarify. I understood what everyone said.	VS —— (OK) —— NW A couple of people did ask someone to give examples and explain their thinking.
Ask others what they think so we hear from all participants.	(VS) —— OK —— NW I was so proud. I was nervous, but Luiz hadn't said anything so I asked him what he thought and he told us!	VS —— OK —— (NW) I'm the only one who asked someone what they thought.

of their learning target ("I understand that building on each other's ideas helps create a collaborative discussion") and two associated success criteria ("I can ask my classmates questions to better understand their ideas" and "I can link my ideas to my classmates' ideas using those linking phrases"). The students completed a self-reflection log by responding to the following questions (Teaching Channel, 2015):

- What examples of positive ways of participating in a collaborative discussion did we find as a class?
- Did I use any of these examples when I participated in the discussion? Please describe how you did this.

- How did I do with meeting the success criteria?
- How can I improve my participation in a collaborative discussion? List at least two ways.

Lead the group in assessing collaborative processes. Another approach to student reflection is to use discussion itself as a way to debrief the effectiveness of the class discourse. In a teacher-guided discussion, the teacher can pose a number of prepared questions to the class, providing an opportunity for each student to reflect on and assess the group's collective performance. Again, the prompts for such a debrief would vary, depending on which skills the class is working to develop. In the video clip of Ms. Bouchard's 4th grade class, she engaged the whole class in a reflective dialogue after the students had responded individually to prompts. She asked, "What do you think we need to do before we answer the next question? What are we going to work on as a class? [pause] Charlie?" Charlie responded, "Try to ask one another more questions, because we're pretty much all saying our own thing."

In this example, the teacher asked students to reflect individually before sharing their thinking. However, it is possible to effectively engage students in collective thinking without individual reflection. Imagine this: a 9th grade history class has discussed the impact of the Great Depression on the character of those who lived through it. Further imagine that the class focused on the following use-of-knowledge skills:

- Evidences serious preparation for discussion by referring to texts and related research.
- Integrates evidence from multiple sources into one's argument.
- Raises questions related to the ideas presented in a text.

In a class debrief, the teacher might decide to pose the following questions:

- One of our skill areas for improvement related to the referencing of multiple texts and other sources throughout our discussion. What evidence can you offer that many of you brought that skill into today's discussion?
- To what extent were you and other members of the class able to relate information from these multiple sources into your arguments?

- How many of you questioned the ideas presented in a text? Why do you think this is a difficult skill to master?

The questions for reflective dialogue will vary from discussion to discussion, depending on the focus and purpose of the discussion. Assuming this 9th grade class has made significant progress in the use of collaborative skills for discussion, the teacher will occasionally refocus students on these skills to keep them on everyone's radar. For example, during a future discussion, the teacher might say, "I notice that many of you are building on one another's ideas and posing questions to clarify." This oral reflection provides formative feedback to students about their progress in mastering discussion skills.

Reflect on the quality of the focus question and the dynamics of the discussion. Following a class discussion, teachers should reflect both individually and with their colleagues, when possible, about their planning and facilitation of the class discussion. Key questions for individual teacher reflection include the following:

- How did the focus question work for this class? Did it generate the type of thinking I had anticipated? Were there any surprises? How might I revise it for future discussions on this topic?
- How effectively did the opening of the discussion prepare all students to participate?
- What, specifically, did I do to sustain student thinking and talking?
- What else, if anything, might I have done to support and sustain student thinking and talking?
- To what extent did all students appear to be comfortable contributing to the discussion?
- In what ways did students demonstrate respect for one another's points of view?
- What might a visitor to our class have noted about the culture for dialogue?
- To what extent did the students exhibit progress toward identified skills? What evidence supports this assessment?

Teachers can better respond to these questions if they record the class discussion. We highly recommend this practice—if not for every class discussion, at least on a routine basis.

Although an individual teacher can engage in private reflection about a discussion, reflection can be more powerful and productive when done collaboratively by a group of colleagues within a professional learning community, grade-level team, or disciplinary team. It's helpful if two teachers are facilitating a discussion around the same question and can compare student responses and interactions. This, of course, is not always possible. Even if your colleague has not facilitated the same discussion on the same day as you, a reflection partner or partners can help each of us take our retrospective thinking to deeper levels.

Reflection should lead students and teachers alike to set goals for future discussions. Students should be encouraged to set new goals after reflecting on their participation in a given discussion. Teachers can formulate new goals for themselves and for their students.

Coaching the Process

Teacher-guided discussion is the venue in which teachers model, scaffold, and otherwise coach students in the skills and dispositions they can use to become more proficient as thoughtful speakers and respectful listeners. Teachers can use the Stages of the Discussion Process (see Figure 3.1 on page 63) to create and execute a game plan that will support student development of targeted skills and dispositions. The tools and strategies associated with each of the five stages of this process can support teachers as they plan and facilitate discussions designed to deepen student learning of content while building student capacity to discuss skillfully without overt teacher guidance.

Teacher-guided discussion also introduces a pattern that students will discern when participating in structured small-group and student-driven discussions. The roles and responsibilities of both teacher and students change in the structured small-group and student-driven settings. Teachers move out of action, assuming the role of observer, supporter, and monitor. Students become increasingly responsible for initiating and sustaining the discussion process, for monitoring their own and their peers' use of targeted skills and dispositions, and for owning their learning and contributing to the learning of others in their classroom community.

Reflecting and Connecting

In this chapter, we examined five stages of discussion—from planning to reflection. Think about the students in your classes and your colleagues as you reflect on the following questions:

- **Planning:** What might be the advantages of collaborative planning for discussions? With which colleagues in your school might you collaborate in thinking about and planning for more effective use of classroom discussions? What about engaging students in the planning process? How might you incorporate student voice?
- **Opening:** What do you believe to be the most important reasons for planning an opening to a discussion? Given the age and developmental level of your students, what might an opening in your classroom look and sound like?
- **Sustaining:** Reflect on your current approach to guiding a discussion. What new insights did you have as you read about sustaining a discussion?
- **Closing:** What is your view of "closing" a discussion? How often do your students leave a discussion with more questions to ponder?
- **Reflecting:** In what ways can you use reflection as a type of formative feedback to ensure that students progress in developing discussion skills? How can reflection help you hone your skills in planning and guiding a discussion?

When might you use teacher-guided discussions with your students?

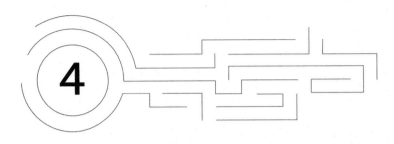

Structured Small-Group Discussion: Using Protocols to Scaffold Skills for Discussion

How can we strategically use small-group structures to develop student discussion skills?

The kindergarten children gather excitedly to hear their teacher read. Each sits on a square on the large rug, wiggling a bit. "Stand and give a hug to your partner. Say hello in your partner voice," Ms. Glass says. Every child stands, faces a partner who is seated in the adjoining square, and gives a hug. They speak to one another in quiet voices. "Thank you," says Ms. Glass. "Now sit down." Ms. Glass pauses while the children settle and continues, "I'm going to read a book. As you listen to the story, use your zero-level voice." She points to the "0" on a voice-level wall chart (see Figure 4.1). "What does a level-zero voice mean?" The children want to answer, but they remember the classroom rule to not raise hands. One or two sit on their hands so as not to raise them. Ms. Glass calls on Ian, who responds, "A zero-level voice means we're not talking at all." Ms. Glass pauses briefly to model thinking about what Ian has said, then addresses the class: "Show me if you agree." All the children give a thumbs-up signal. "OK. Let's start our new book."

Figure 4.1 | **Range of Classroom Voice Levels**

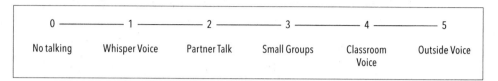

"Look at the picture on the front of the book," Ms. Glass says as she points again to the zero-level voice on the chart and places her finger on her lips to cue her students that this is a question she wants them to think about and answer to themselves. "Study the picture carefully and think: What might this book be about? Be ready to give a reason for your prediction." Ms. Glass waits in silence while the children study the picture and think about her question, then continues, "Talk to your partner about your answer." All students stand and face their partners, each talking and listening. Ms. Glass moves among the students as she listens in on their conversations.

"Thank you for using your level-two voices—your partner voices," she says. "Sit down and we'll hear what you were thinking. When I call on you to share, remember to use your classroom voice." Ms. Glass points to the number "4" on the wall chart, pauses to get everyone's attention, and asks, "What was your prediction?" She pauses again. "Jessie?" The class turns to Jessie and listens to her response: "We think the story is going to be about covered wagons because we see a family in the wagon pulled by horses." A comfortable pause is followed by a comment from a second student: "We saw the same thing. And we thought the story would be about the little girls walking behind the wagon." After another pause, the student adds, "We think they may get lost. They are looking at the flowers in the field. They aren't paying attention to their mom and dad." Ms. Glass takes comments from two other students—each of whom builds on previous comments—and then begins to read the book. She stops four more times to pose questions. With each question, she has the children stand, talk with their partners, and share with the large group.

Does this vignette describe a "discussion"? Think about the definition for discussion that we offered in Chapter 2: *Discussion is a process through which individual students give voice to their thoughts in a disciplined manner as they interact with others to make meaning and advance individual and collective understanding of the issue in question.* Pairs of students used a structured process to think, speak, and listen, which resulted in individual and collective meaning-making about the story to which they were listening. This kindergarten teacher was scaffolding important discussion skills for these young students while engaging them in speculative thinking. Our view is that this does qualify as discussion, a discussion scaffolded by a protocol within a small-group structure.

Throughout this chapter, we look at structures for small-group, student-to-student discussions that can facilitate learning and the development of discussion skills. Consider the description of Ms. Glass's kindergarten classroom. Which of the following purposes of questioning do you think were accomplished? (See Figure 1.1 on page 15 to review the purposes of questioning in recitation and discussion.)

- Did students make personal meaning? Connect to prior knowledge?
- Did they extend or deepen their thinking?
- Did students listen to, understand, and appreciate diverse points of view?
- Did they reflect on their own and others' beliefs?
- Were students developing a life skill important for working in groups?

Ms. Glass's use of Think-Pair-Share, with students responding to an open-ended, predictive question, accomplishes most of these purposes—and engages all students in talking and listening to one another. Her skillful use of "think times," and the expectation that all students are to formulate a response and be ready to answer, reinforces student engagement and student thinking. At the same time, the structure itself helps students develop important social skills (talking and listening to peers) and cognitive skills (making predictions and offering reasons for them), which prepares them to discuss more rigorous questions in a whole-group setting. As the structure is used repeatedly, and as the teacher intentionally calls attention to the children's use of these skills, the hope is that students will transfer them to other classroom interactions and to settings beyond the classroom.

Small-group structures, such as Think-Pair-Share, are particularly useful for engaging students and holding each one accountable for preparing a response to every question (Walsh & Sattes, 2005, 2011). Unlike the traditional classroom response format, in which one student at a time volunteers and answers, structured small-group formats have the potential to engage every student in a classroom in thinking, speaking, listening, and collaborating with classmates—and these formats can serve multiple purposes. Teachers often use them in recitations to review and check for understanding. We featured them in Chapter 3 as a means to activate discussions and jump-start student talk when a discussion lags. However, many of these structures can also serve as "containers" for true discussion when teachers employ them in tandem with focus questions that prompt student thinking to deepen understanding and make meaning (beyond simple recall). In this chapter we will feature small-group structures that encourage students to talk to one another (rather than to the teacher); listen carefully to one another while questioning and valuing different points of view; and use their knowledge to deepen understanding.

So how do we define structured small-group discussion? We view it as the setting in which protocols, or carefully defined procedures, govern the interactions of a limited number of students and support focused thinking and intentional use of discussion skills. While the choice of protocol is the most obvious distinction characterizing any given small-group structure, other structural features also affect the nature and quality of student interactions. These include group size, group composition, roles and responsibilities for group members, and group ground rules. Teachers make decisions about the protocol and the other four structural characteristics by reference to learning targets—both content learning targets and process targets related to student development of skills and dispositions for discussion.

The group structures that we review in this chapter are first presented in Figure 4.2, in five groups or organizers, each representing a cluster of skills for discussion. These five organizers are

1. Developing accountability to speak,

2. Learning to listen through silence,

3. Learning to appreciate multiple points of view and deepen understanding of text,

4. Learning to agree and disagree respectfully, and

5. Learning to question.

These organizers demonstrate the interaction among the disparate skills across our three categories of skills (social, cognitive, and use of knowledge). Students must draw from all three skill sets when participating in a disciplined and thoughtful small-group discussion; the skills are interdependent and mutually reinforcing.

We have selected 16 small-group structures, each of which we believe can be harnessed to enhance student discussion skills. To accomplish this end, teachers must be very intentional in matching protocol to instructional purpose and very transparent with students about expectations for the use of specific skills. We agree with the authors of *Making Thinking Visible* that the repeated and consistent use of selected protocols will help students develop and refine cognitive skills (Ritchhart, Church, & Morrison, 2011); we also believe this approach can develop social and use-of-knowledge skills.

The structures in Figure 4.2 do not constitute an exhaustive list, but they promote a variety of instructional purposes and help students develop the discussion skills presented in Chapter 2. All of these protocols use questioning to promote discussion and serve the following purposes:

- Help students learn and retain important content by making meaning through speaking and listening to peers—thereby clarifying their own thinking.
- Provide information to teachers about students' level of understanding (or misconceptions) so teachers can purposefully plan next steps.
- Engage students in thinking beyond the "remember" level of cognition.

- Scaffold and provide practice in important social and cognitive skills required for discussions.
- Establish the expectation of equity in student response opportunities.
- Sustain a culture of thoughtfulness and safety, helping students experience a truly risk-free classroom environment.

Another benefit associated with the use of small-group structures is the opportunity for teacher monitoring and coaching of individuals and groups. As teachers walk around the classroom, listening in on student dialogue, they can provide on-the-spot coaching by making comments and using other scaffolds described in Chapter 3. Additionally, teachers can formatively assess both student understanding of content and their use of discussion skills, taking notes for later feedback to students and for planning next steps.

The use of structured small groups also allows the flexibility for differentiation when needed. For example, the teacher can assign different reading passages to match reading levels of different groups of students; plan in advance to work with a group of students who need intensive coaching in content; or allow students who have mastered core knowledge and skills to engage in a more open, student-driven discussion to go deeper in their thinking.

Beginning with Pairs: Building Accountability to Speak

The scenario at the beginning of this chapter demonstrates the use of Think-Pair-Share in a kindergarten classroom, but this small-group structure can be used for any grade or subject area. It's useful for helping students make personal meaning as they process information from a text, teacher lecture, video, or problem. It's very appropriate to use with students who are learning how to discuss. Once students understand Think-Pair-Share, they know the routine involves thinking quietly about their own answers and, on the teacher's cue, sharing their responses with a partner. They learn to take responsibility for thinking of their own answers and for expressing their ideas clearly as they speak to a classmate. Further, they learn to listen as their partner speaks and, with guidance from their teacher, to ask questions so they fully understand their partner's comments. In many classrooms, this new way of interacting is quite a departure

Figure 4.2 | **Protocols Organized by Relationship to Discussion Skills**

Clusters of Skills and Related Protocols	Social Skills	Cognitive Skills	Use-of-Knowledge Skills
Developing Accountability to Speak Think-Pair-Share, Read-Write-Pair-Share	• Speaks to classmates (not just to the teacher) • Contributes to the discussion so others can learn from him or her • Expresses own ideas clearly • Listens actively (i.e., looks at speaking student and gives nonverbal cues that one is paying attention) • Accurately paraphrases what another student says • "Piggybacks" and elaborates on classmates' comments	• Relates prior knowledge (both academic and personal) to the topic of discussion • Offers reasons and textual evidence to support one's own point of view • Poses questions to clarify the thinking or reasoning behind partner's comment • Contributes to the building of a collaborative solution	• Draws relevant information from prior learning, other content areas, and out-of-school sources • Relates comments to the subject or question for discussion; does not get off topic • When asked, cites specific evidence from text or other source
Learning to Listen through Silence Ink Think, Affinity Mapping	• Uses silence to think about the meaning of others' comments and to compare to own thinking • Expresses own ideas clearly (in writing, initially) • "Piggybacks" and elaborates on classmates' comments	• Identifies similarities and differences between own and others' ideas • Relates prior knowledge to the topic • Contributes to the building of a collaborative solution	• Draws relevant information from prior learning, other content, and out-of-school experiences • Relates comments to the subject or question for discussion; does not get off topic
Learning to Appreciate Multiple Points of View and Deepen Understanding of Text Say Something, The Final Word, Save the Last Word for Me, Sentence-Phrase-Word, Four-Square Share	• Speaks to classmates (not just to teacher) • Remains open to ideas that are different from one's own • "Piggybacks" and elaborates on classmates' comments • Disagrees in a civil and respectful manner • Uses silence after a classmate stops speaking to think about what was said and to compare those thoughts to own • Contributes to the discussion so others can learn from him or her • Expresses own ideas clearly • Speaks at length so thinking is visible to others • Paraphrases portions of a text	• Identifies similarities and differences between one's own ideas and those of others • Relates prior knowledge to text • Offers reasons and textual evidence to support one's own point of view • Poses questions to clarify and better understand a text • Asks "what if" questions to encourage divergent thinking • Suspends judgment while listening to interpretation from a classmate • Draws inferences from different speakers' ideas that take the conversation to a deeper level • Contributes to the building of a collaborative solution (or understanding)	• Cites specific evidence from text or other sources • Relates comments to subject or question for discussion; does not get off topic • Draws relevant information from prior learning and personal experiences

| Learning to Agree and Disagree Respectfully

People-Graph, Data on Display, Table Rounds | • Speaks to classmates (not just to the teacher)
• Contributes to the discussion so others can learn from him or her
• Expresses own ideas clearly
• Accurately paraphrases what another student says
• Remains open to ideas that are different from one's own
• Disagrees in a civil and respectful manner | • Identifies similarities and differences between own and others' ideas
• Relates prior knowledge to the topic of discussion
• Analyzes and evaluates information from different sources
• Offers reasons and textual evidence to support own point of view
• Asks questions to identify a speaker's assumptions
• Poses questions to clarify the thinking behind an argument or conclusion
• Draws inferences from different speakers' ideas that take the conversation to a deeper level
• Suspends judgment while listening to a new solution or interpretation from a classmate | • Cites information sources
• Evaluates the credibility of information sources
• Relates comments to the subject for discussion
• Uses academic vocabulary and the language of the discipline
• Draws relevant information from prior learning in subject area, from other content areas, and from out-of-school sources
• Reflects on and evaluates personal beliefs or positions on issues in relation to ideas offered in a discussion
• Connects current social, economic, or cultural phenomena to academic content on which discussion is focused |
| Learning to Question

See-Think-Wonder, Think-Puzzle-Explore, IQ Pairs, Questioning Circle | • Speaks to classmates as well as to teacher
• Speaks clearly and loudly enough that everyone can hear
• Expresses own ideas clearly
• Uses silence after a classmate stops speaking to think about what was said and to compare those thoughts to own
• Waits before adding own ideas
• "Piggybacks" and elaborates on classmates' comments | • Poses questions to clarify and better understand the substance of a topic or text
• Asks questions when curious
• Poses questions to clarify the thinking behind an argument or conclusion
• Asks "what if" questions to encourage divergent thinking
• Suspends judgment while listening to a new solution or interpretation from a classmate | • Relates prior knowledge to the topic of discussion
• Draws relevant information from prior learning
• Reflects on and evaluates personal beliefs or positions on issues in relation to ideas offered in a discussion
• Relates comments to the subject or question for discussion; does not get off topic |

from the traditional classroom situation in which teachers do most of the talking and asking. To use Think-Pair-Share successfully, teachers will need to lay the groundwork.

Consider how Ms. Glass worked to establish successful pair talk prior to the scenario that opened this chapter. Early in the school year, as she began using Think-Pair-Share, she thought about how to partner students. She wanted heterogeneous academic pairs and matched gender so that her kindergarteners would feel comfortable speaking to their partners. She made a list of students—by performance in reading and English language arts—and paired a girl from the upper third of students with a girl from the middle group. She paired a boy from the middle group with a boy from the lowest-performing group.

In Ms. Glass's early use of Think-Pair-Share, to scaffold students' taking responsibility for speaking and listening, she numbered each student in a pair as a "1" or a "2." After posing a question and allowing time for all to think, she cued the 1's to speak, allowed time, and then signaled the 2's to speak, ensuring that every student had the opportunity to express a point of view. To reinforce listening to understand, she called on students during whole-group discussion to share what their partners had said. After several months of this scaffolding, the students transitioned to talking together (as opposed to turn talking) during pair talk. They had learned to speak and listen thoughtfully—two basic social skills for discussions in and out of school.

A brief whole-group, teacher-guided discussion might follow after Ms. Glass reads the book to the students several times so that they understand the plot and characters and have adequate background knowledge about the historical times in which the action occurred. But for on-the-spot processing of information, Ms. Glass poses questions that have more than one correct answer and makes sure her questions require thought. In groups of two, as is routine after a teacher question in this classroom, every student is fully engaged: both listening and speaking.

As you may recall, Ms. Glass asks her students to stand each time they talk in pairs. Perhaps you wondered, "Why have them stand? Doesn't that take a lot of time?" Ms. Glass's reasoning is that kindergarteners like to move, and the physical activity of changing positions provides an outlet for their energy. In addition, she finds that when the children stand, she is able to listen to their conversations without having to kneel down and get back up as she moves from pair to pair. So incorporating physical activity into Think-Pair-Share is a win-win solution.

Teachers know it's important to stop frequently while reading a book so they can pose questions to help students make predictions, consider consequences, understand characters and plot lines, and make personal meaning. But if those questions elicit a response from only one student—as is the case in traditional classrooms where recitation is the primary questioning format—not every student formulates or provides a response. Also, teachers don't learn how most students are thinking and comprehending, and students miss the chance to make their own meaning by thinking aloud and listening to another person. Paired discussion (beginning with Think-Pair-Share) is fundamental to becoming skilled at larger group discussions.

Think-Pair-Share can be adapted to suit the needs of students in higher grade levels. For example, in Read-Write-Pair-Share, every student reads a short passage from a text, thinks about a teacher-posed question related to the text, reflects and writes a response, pairs with a partner to talk about and compare thoughts, and then shares responses with the larger group. An excellent precursor to large-group discussion—or to further writing—this opportunity to talk "primes the pump" of student thinking before they verbalize to the larger group or commit thoughts to paper. If students are paired heterogeneously, such a strategy can ensure that students develop better understanding of the passage (by listening to partners) and are prepared to contribute their best thinking to a group discussion.

Learning to Listen Carefully Through Silence

Some small-group protocols use silence for part of the initial "discussion." We will describe two such protocols. Both help students sharpen at least two social skills: (1) listening to classmates (by using silence to think about classmates' responses and compare them to one's own thinking) and (2) collaboration (by piggybacking and elaborating on classmates' comments).

Brief periods of intentional silence after a question and after a response were introduced in Chapter 1 as "think times." A necessary part of the re-culturing of a classroom to support thoughtful discussion is adoption of the following norm:

Use silence during a discussion to process what others have said, to rethink your own position, and to consolidate thinking.

Several benefits of consistent use of think times 1 and 2 are reported in research: more students respond to questions; student responses are lengthier and more thoughtful; students respond at higher cognitive levels; and students pose more questions (Rowe, 1986). All of these outcomes are valuable for productive discussions. During think times, speakers can complete their responses without interruption, and listeners can process what was said and consider whether they agree or disagree, and why.

We advocate teaching students "the what, the why, and the how" of think times so that students understand how to use these moments of silence productively (Walsh & Sattes, 2011). We have learned that think times cannot be done without students' involvement and commitment. Teachers and students alike find the pause after someone responds (think time 2) especially difficult to learn and use consistently. The two protocols presented here are useful in helping students understand the value of silence for deeper thinking. The silence associated with these protocols exceeds the usual three- to five-second think times by several minutes. Both protocols begin with silent generation of ideas and engage students in three fundamental tasks: generating ideas in response to a prompt or a question, sorting ideas into categories, and naming the categories with a one- to three-word label.

Ink Think

Ink Think can be used with virtually any subject area: science, math, English language arts, social studies, art, music, or foreign language. Students typically review and silently record their thoughts about one or more questions. They gather in groups before a large sheet of paper (on the wall, table, or desks) and record their ideas. They do this silently—without speaking—while they read one another's ideas and build on them. Their "mind map" creation shows connections between ideas as they add them. In some cases, with multiple questions, groups progress to the next station, read the first group's writing, mark ideas with a check or plus ("I agree") or question mark ("I wonder about this") and then add their own ideas. The silence seems to increase students' listening to understand. This is the generation of ideas phase. As they return to their original station, students may speak to one another to review the ideas and cluster them into main concepts (the sorting phase). Finally, together, they name each cluster. Generate/sort/name is a useful template that students can use to think collaboratively in response to a prompt.

Ms. Stevenson's 1st grade class (PS 208, Brooklyn, NY) used Ink Think to generate ideas (without grouping and naming) to help students explore more deeply three math concepts: taller, shorter, and longer. The teacher posted the question on an interactive whiteboard ("How can you demonstrate longer? Shorter? Taller?"), along with the directions for Ink Think. Some students drew pictures illustrating their understanding of the concepts; others wrote words or examples. The students were so proud of their work as they shared it with others in their class!

In a more complex application, imagine a middle school social studies class in which the focus is on learning to read informational texts, identifying central and supporting ideas, and summarizing the reading (CCSS-ELA.RI.8.2). The content focus of the lesson is the U.S. civil rights movement of the 1960s. The teacher has selected four powerful readings—each with a slightly different point of view and emphasis—and assigned one of the readings to each class member. After the students complete their readings, they respond individually in writing to the following question:

> In your assigned reading, what were the author's main ideas related to the civil rights movement in this country? Be specific. Be ready to support your choices with text from your reading.

After students have time to reflect individually, they gather in small groups of four to six students, each of whom has read the same assignment. Each student uses a marker to silently record on a wall chart the main ideas they garnered from the reading. They read other students' ideas and extend them, if appropriate, by adding examples or alternative words or concepts. They draw dotted lines between similar ideas to show connections, thereby creating a visual web of ideas. The amount of time allotted to this part of the small-group structure can vary. In this case, the teacher allows three to four minutes because the readings are complex and the students are old enough to actively use this silence (extended "think time") to go deeper with their own thinking and to build on one another's ideas.

"Students take active responsibility for their learning during Ink Think. They like the movement and the idea that they can agree or disagree with other's responses. The evidence of thinking and learning is visible, and I love that. Overall, students have been very receptive. They understand that they all need time to think. [As a consequence of Ink Think], I have had students tell others that they need to wait because some students were still thinking. In the past, students sometimes tried to get through the day by letting other students answer questions. This year, students respond in discussions; they know that the expectation is for everyone to have a response."

—Reflections from Ms. Zimmerman, 3rd grade English, Reading, and Social Studies Teacher, Wiederstein Elementary School, Cibolo, Texas

When the teacher calls time, group members review what has been written on their paper to identify clusters of related ideas. The thinking that was made visible as students wrote in silence is now extended as they discuss how ideas relate to one another and form bigger ideas. These discrete groups of ideas serve as the group's summary of their reading. In preparation for sharing with the entire class, groups create names (one to three words) for each category of ideas. For example, one group clustered their ideas and created the following "big ideas": discrimination, Jim Crow laws, difficult change, segregation in schools, civil disobedience, police violence, and voting rights.

Finally, as each group reports a summary of its reading passage, students listen and individually record ideas that are similar to and different from the ideas they identified from their own group's reading. This activity generates fodder for a small- or large-group discussion, as students consider questions like these: *What main ideas occurred in most of the readings? What ideas did you see that were unique to a single reading? Speculate on why that author may have highlighted a particular idea when none of the other writers did.*

An alternative to the above procedure is to have students regroup for the final step of sharing, with each new group including at least one student representative from each of the four original teams. These reconfigured groups move from station to station. The students who participated in the creation of the visual at each given station share a summary of their group's thinking. After each group has rotated through all stations, members discuss which ideas appeared in several readings and which ideas were unique to a single reading—and they speculate as to why.

When students debrief this type of learning experience, they readily see the benefits of learning with peers as opposed to learning in isolation. They recognize that students who read the same passage may come away with different understandings and insights, based on the point of view that each brings to the text from their own experiences and beliefs (see the Ladder of Inferences in Chapter 2 on p. 36). Students understand that their thinking is enhanced when they listen to others' ideas. They also gain insight into the value of silence as a way to extend their thinking and listening skills. Participation in Ink Think increases students' awareness of the value of think times; the silence helps them "listen" better to one another; the pausing to think carries over into other classroom discussions.

"Only a handful of students participate in the traditional classroom question/answer routine. When I use Ink Think, they *all* participate—and they enjoy feeling like they have the opportunity and responsibility to give input. Sometimes I leave their Ink Think thoughts up for a week or two. Students just get very comfortable randomly adding responses. It generates conversation about whatever theme we're talking about.

continued

As an English teacher, I can't stress the importance of communication and respectful and mindful self-expression enough. Strategies such as Ink Think help to build student-to-student and teacher-to-student communities. It helps to create a safe haven for self-reflection and expression. The point is to motivate students to sit longer with a topic and explore more deeply, preparing to make a viable contribution to classroom discussion. It's a beautiful thing when a student realizes his or her own thoughts are powerful and then feels comfortable enough to speak the magic of his or her own voice. That is the benefit of using these sorts of strategies."

—Reflections from Carie Novikoff, English Language Arts Teacher, Clemens High School, Schertz, Texas

Affinity Mapping

Affinity Mapping (another Generate-Sort-Name activity) is most often used to surface prior knowledge at the beginning of a unit or to consolidate learning and review at the end of a content unit. Here's how it might look in a 3rd grade science lesson where students are attempting to achieve the "distinguished" category of performance for this standard: *Create a method of classification for various organisms and evaluate how well structures are adapted to specific environments.*

The teacher poses the first question: *Generate a list of living things. Write each example on a separate sticky note.* Every student individually and silently generates the names of living things and writes each individual idea legibly on a separate sticky note. Then, in groups of four to six students, they silently post their sticky notes onto a large paper in order to answer the following question: *Imagine that your group is responsible for creating a classification system—that is, a way of sorting living things into meaningful categories of similar objects. How would you group your living things together, and why?*

As students post in silence, they read others' ideas and group them into like categories, adding ideas as they read and reflect on the postings. It never fails that during this time of silence, questions arise that can be discussed in the next step (e.g.,"Why did she group that with this?" "How are those two related—or are they?"). When time is called, the students talk to one another as they finalize their groupings of ideas, moving sticky notes around to form categories they can all agree are discrete. They have to discuss to come to common understandings about decisions to classify living organisms. As they do this, they may add more sticky notes to create categories that aren't represented. Once students have completed the classification (or sorting) step, they name each category.

When Affinity Mapping is used at the beginning of a unit, as in this example, the teacher learns much about students' current understanding of the topic (in this case, categories of living things—do the students list mammals, reptiles, fish, birds, trees, flowers, and bacteria?). The teacher also learns about students' misconceptions (e.g., do the students forget major categories, such as people and plants? Or include nonliving things such as rocks, dirt, and cars?).

Learning to Appreciate Multiple Points of View and Deepen Understanding of Text or Other Media

Reading comprehension is fundamental to learning in all subjects. Deep comprehension involves making personal meaning, as students connect what they already know to what they are reading. This is best done by allowing readers the opportunity to make personal meaning during a time of quiet reading and reflection prior to the sharing of their thinking with one another. Sharing with classmates serves two primary purposes: individual accountability for reading and thinking and the opportunity to extend learning through speaking and listening. Hammond and Nessel (2011) summarize Vygotsky's thinking about the relationship among thinking, speaking, and learning: "Learners must talk in order to learn: to the teacher, to each other, and to themselves" (p. 20).

The five protocols we describe in this section encourage exploration and understanding of text; however, any of them could also be used to deepen understanding about a piece of visual art or music, the results of a science lab experiment, or a math problem or concept. These protocols help students read with a purpose, discuss text through a structured process, and learn that others have different interpretations of the reading. Hearing different points of view stretches each student's understanding.

Research reports that good readers are more apt than poor readers to select more information from a text to remember; additionally, the information they select is more likely to be seen as important to teachers (Hammond & Nessel, 2011). This research has implications for grouping students in text-based discussion structures. It would appear that grouping heterogeneously by reading ability might give poorer readers insights into what is important from a text, ideas they may not be quick to pick up on their own.

Say Something

Say Something is a simple paired activity that's particularly useful in helping students process lists or dense text. In pairs, students silently read an assigned passage, then turn and say something to their partners about what they have read: what it means to them, what questions it raises for them, or in what ways they agree or disagree with the text. Typically, after one reading and pair sharing, the teacher invites whole-group sharing, asking students, "What did you hear your partner say?" and "Do you agree or disagree, and why?"

Once students have learned to read accountably—knowing they need to read for comprehension so they can say something about what they have read—teachers can add a requirement: identifying the part of the text that gave rise to the student's question or idea. Beyond listening carefully, partners are encouraged to ask each other, "What part of the paragraph caused you to wonder that?" or "What, in the text, led you to that conclusion?" In short, this structure can help build the important skills of active listening, asking questions to better understand the speaker's point of view, and encouraging peers to cite textual evidence for their comments.

Once students learn the basics of reading and turn talking about the meaning of a passage, the stage is set for discussion. After each student says something, the pair discusses the shared ideas: Do we understand what the text is communicating? Do we understand the vocabulary? Are both ideas (if different) supported by the text? Can we agree on a summary statement of this reading (or poem, artwork, etc.)?

The Final Word

The Final Word is a text-based structure that serves many purposes, among them the scaffolding of the following student skills: (1) reading for understanding and (2) learning to appreciate different points of view that spring from a single reading passage. This protocol from the National School Reform Faculty (http://www.nsrfharmony.org/free-resources/protocols/text) also helps to build the skills of (3) speaking at length and making thinking visible, (4) paraphrasing selected text, and (5) assuring equity of participation. Listening skills are reinforced as students (6) intentionally use silence (only one student speaks at a time) to compare their own thoughts to those of the speaker. Here's how the protocol works:

- Ahead of time: Read a passage and find two to three important ideas worthy of discussion.
- In groups of three to five (four is our favorite size), seated so that all can see and hear others, select a *facilitator* (to ensure fidelity to the protocol) and a *timekeeper* (to alert speakers when their time has elapsed).
- Throughout the protocol, when one person is speaking, everyone else is listening. There are no back-and-forth discussions, and no interruptions of the speaker. All listen attentively.
- A volunteer begins by introducing an idea and pointing to its location in the text. The speaker has two minutes in which to talk about the idea—explaining why he or she believes it is important, agreeing or disagreeing with the author, or posing a question related to the idea.
- Every other group member, in turn, comments on the speaker's idea for no more than one minute—adding to, clarifying, presenting a different point of view, and so forth.
- When all have addressed the idea, the initial speaker has up to one minute for "the final word." This is an opportunity for the speaker to clarify his thinking about the idea he introduced.
- In turn, each group member introduces an idea, speaks, and listens as others discuss it.

The most powerful outcome of this protocol is the generation of different points of view on a topic. Because only one person speaks at a time, and others in the group are expected to respond when their time comes, all students are likely to listen and to compare what is said to what they were thinking. Although the protocol associated with the Final Word might seem unnatural at first, the benefits outweigh any initial discomfort.

What is the value of text-based protocols?

The following are examples of reflective feedback from participants who used the Final World to engage in small-group sharing:

- "Everyone gets to participate equally; no one can dominate the group's discussion."
- "Everyone listened to me!"
- "I don't usually like to say anything in a group so I was nervous. But I did it and it got easier each time I had to speak."
- "I finally got to finish a thought without being interrupted."
- "I didn't think I could talk for a whole minute, but I did it."
- "It makes you think; you have to think about what you think—so you can talk about it."
- "Everyone was so respectful. The quiet helps us all pay attention and concentrate on what someone is saying. The silence is hard to do, but it works to make you listen and hear others."

Save the Last Word for Me

Save the Last Word for Me is similar to the Final Word, with a few modifications: The first volunteer contributes an idea he or she found interesting while reading a text, pointing to the position in the text where the excerpt is located and reads it aloud to classmates. The student does not comment on the selection at this point but listens as other group members speak in turn about the idea. Time limits on speaking are optional and depend on the composition of the class. The opportunity to give "the last word" passes to the initiator of the idea after other group members have spoken. This student incorporates what others have said into his or her thinking. Using the same protocol, other group members, in turn, introduce an idea from the text.

All three of these protocols—Say Something, the Final Word, and Save the Last Word for Me—ensure that no two students speak at the same time. One teacher who uses these protocols commented, "The sound in the classroom contains a kind of energy that lets me know students are listening to one another and are thinking. I love it!"

Four-Square Share

Four-Square Share is another small-group structure that enables students to learn from others' perspectives. Students prepare by reading a passage and writing a brief summary of the main ideas. They then form groups of four as directed by the teacher. One at a time, students share their summaries with other group members. As each student speaks, others listen and take notes. After all group members share, they engage in a short discussion, looking for common ideas across the group as well as pertinent ideas that were not previously mentioned. Finally, each student individually writes a one- or two-sentence summary, drawing relevant ideas from the other students. Teachers can collect each student's work to obtain valuable formative feedback related to three important skills: how well students independently understood the passage, listened to and understood one another, and incorporated ideas from others into their own final synthesis.

Sentence-Phrase-Word

Yet another protocol that supports meaningful structured small-group discussion is Sentence-Phrase-Word, described in *Making Thinking Visible* (Ritchhart et al., 2011). As students read an assigned text, they identify important ideas. When they finish, they record or highlight three things: (1) a sentence that is important to the meaning of the passage, (2) a phrase that is meaningful

Examples of Four-Square Share

The 2nd graders in Ms. Marrotta's class, PS 39, Staten Island, New York, read an article about the construction of the Empire State Building and another article about the bridges in New York City. They each wrote a summary of their reading in the top left corner of their papers; shared with others in their group (as listeners took notes in one of the four corners of their papers); and discussed what they each had learned from the passage and from one another. After the sharing and discussion, each student individually wrote a second summary (in a box in the middle of the page) and turned it in to the teacher. The teacher shared two examples with us, where it was clear that the students had listened carefully to what other group members said. In one, a student included many examples from other students' summaries in her final summary. In another example, the group discussion enabled the student to better understand the main idea of the passage. He had initially thought the passage was about specific tunnels and bridges in New York. After hearing other students' summaries, he understood the passage was about the importance of bridges and tunnels in connecting the boroughs of the city.

to them, and (3) a word in the passage that seems particularly powerful, summarizes the reading, or captures the main idea. Students meet in groups of four. The group facilitator asks one student to share his or her selected sentence, point to where it can be found in the passage, and explain why that specific sentence was selected. The other group members read the sentence in their text and compare it (silently) to their own choices. This process is repeated until all four group members have shared a sentence. The facilitator then leads the group in discussing questions such as these: *What commonalities do these sentences have, if any? What is the common thread? Which one of the sentences best speak to the meaning of the passage?* After discussion, the teacher may ask each group to reach consensus regarding the sentence that best embodies the meaning of the passage and to have the group recorder write it on paper to share with the rest of the class. Students use the same process to share their phrases and words, with discussion following each round of sharing. Finally, the group looks back at the reading and asks, *Did we miss any of the major points of this reading? Do we want to add a word or a phrase to our discussion summary?*

Learning to Agree and Disagree Respectfully

If students have trouble knowing how to disagree respectfully, these three protocols—People-Graph, Data on Display, and Table Rounds—can help them see and respect different and legitimate points of view. All are very good strategies for generating small-group discussion around controversial issues. They can also prepare students for whole-group discussion, as was illustrated with People-Graph in Chapter 3. Additionally, these protocols scaffold important cognitive skills: identification of similarities and differences between one's own ideas and others', asking questions to identify a speaker's assumptions, and learning to cite reliable information sources to defend one's point of view. The Ladder of Inferences, introduced in Chapter 2, might be helpful to share with students before or after they participate in these protocols.

People-Graph

In a People-Graph, teachers post a controversial statement and, after time for individual reflection, ask students to "take a stand" on a line or continuum that stretches from one end of the room to another, with Strongly Agree at one end and Strongly Disagree at the other. Students can stand at either end or somewhere along the line to represent their opinion. Chapter 3 describes how to use this protocol as the opening of a teacher-guided discussion, but it is also a good process for small-group discussion. For example, imagine posting the following question:

> During the 1940s, '50s, and '60s, the United States employed a draft to fill positions in the armed service that were not filled by volunteers. The draft was ended in 1973; today's military is an all-volunteer service. Do you believe this is a good idea?

Stand on the end of the line where it says "Strongly Agree" if you absolutely agree that volunteers are the best way to staff the military; move to the other end if you "Strongly Disagree" and believe that the draft is the best way to staff the armed services. Move anywhere along the middle to show where you stand between the two positions. Be ready to explain and defend your position.

After students have "taken their stand," they gather with three to four students near them on the People-Graph and articulate their reasons for their position, preparing to share and discuss with the larger group. After the small groups have had sufficient time to document and explain their positions, the teacher asks several of the groups to share with the entire class. At this point, rather than entering a discussion immediately, each listening group gets together to identify (1) questions they would like to pose to the speaking group and (2) data they would like to find that might support or counter the speaking group's position.

The opportunity to conduct research and raise questions counters students' tendencies to base their positions on assumptions and opinions rather than facts. The act of researching questions to support or refute their own and others' positions helps students learn there are multiple points of view for most statements and that people can learn by listening to others. Allow time for students to research their questions so that class members are ready for an in-depth discussion on the topic (possibly the next day).

Data on Display

A second protocol that helps students understand and appreciate differing points of views is Data on Display. The teacher creates four or five statements, worded so that students can agree or disagree. Individually and silently, students read each statement and rate their level of agreement, from 100 percent (Strongly Agree) to 50 percent (both Agree and Disagree) to 0 percent (Strongly Disagree.) Then, using sticky notes (see Figure 4.3), students create bar graphs showing the extent to which they agree with each statement. Individually and silently, students look at the posted results to make personal meaning: *What surprises me? What questions do these data raise for me? What patterns do I see? What can I infer from these data? What conclusions can I draw?* In small groups, students share some of their conclusions and questions. The individual reflection and ranking, followed by small-group discussion, prepares them for a teacher-guided discussion (e.g., a fishbowl or a whole-class discussion).

Data on Display helps students see and understand different points of view. Attempting to understand the bar graphs as group data keeps individuals from "digging in" and arguing for their own points of view. The process almost always results in deeper understanding of the vocabulary used in the initial statements, the shades of differences between opinions, and the value of sharing ideas and backing up points of view.

Building on the example in Chapter 3 about Roosevelt's decision to end American isolationism after the Japanese bombing of Pearl Harbor, imagine that students were asked to consider America's role today in world conflict and to respond about the extent to which they agree with the questions in Figure 4.3.

Figure 4.3 | **Sample Data on Display Bar Graphs**

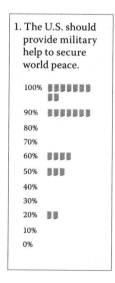
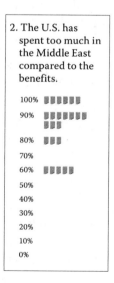
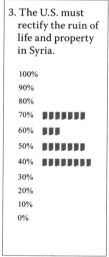
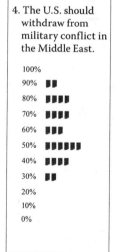

Table Rounds

In Table Rounds, small groups of students listen to, question, and defend different points of view after they have investigated a topic or idea, using either online research or completing teacher-suggested readings. Jackie created Table Rounds for classrooms as a modification of the World Café structure for large groups (Brown & Isaacs, 2005).

As part of the process for preparing for Table Rounds, teachers create four questions for discussion around a common theme or reading. These questions should be authentic, of high interest, and evocative of more than one possible answer. As much as possible, they should relate to students' interests and experiences. Each student will receive all four questions and should have some quiet time to reflect on what they think about the four questions before entering into discussion.

The room is set up with four tables (or groups of desks) so that five to seven students can gather around. On the surface of each table is a "tablecloth"—sheets of easel paper or project paper—on which students can write or draw. All students should have access to crayons or markers to record ideas they individually identify as being central to the discussion.

The teacher assigns students to one of the four tables at which one question serves as the focus for thinking and discussion. The teacher designates one student at each table to serve as "table host" or discussion facilitator. As students discuss the question within their table groups, they listen to one another and contribute to the discussion by verbally agreeing, respectfully disagreeing, or adding questions and insights to extend one another's thinking. Each student uses a marker (or other writing implement) to record key ideas, emerging thoughts, or wonderings. Students are encouraged to use words and graphical and visual displays to represent their thinking. Unlike many small-group structures, Table Rounds does not call for a group recorder, but rather invites every student to contribute key ideas in writing for consideration by future "visitors" to their table.

When the teacher calls time, students stand and move to another table, except the individuals who are serving as the "table hosts." These students remain behind to share the first group's thinking with newcomers. As students change tables, the teacher encourages them to form different groupings by saying, "Try to be seated with mostly new people; avoid being with the same people you were seated with initially." If cliques are a problem, teachers can create movement cards directing each student to join a particular table at each gathering. When the second group gathers at a table, the table host kick-starts the group by sharing the main points that have been made and this group continues to discuss the question, piggybacking on previous comments and adding new ideas of their own. Moves are called twice more, giving every student the opportunity to discuss each of the four questions. Students then move back to their original table and question, where they categorize the main ideas and prepare to share them with the entire group.

Sample Directions for Table Rounds

You will each have the opportunity to discuss four questions—each one with a different group of classmates—as you engage in Table Rounds. Here's the way Table Rounds works:

1. Review the four sets of questions on your handout. Take some time to read through them, think about them, and jot down some responses so you will be ready to discuss each of them with a small group of your classmates.
2. Begin conversations at your assigned table. Respond to the question(s) that match the number of your table.
   a. One person in your group will serve as "Table Host." This individual will facilitate your group's conversation—trying to ensure that you address all questions related to your topic and that all participate.
   b. As you listen and converse, everyone is invited to jot down (or illustrate) big ideas or questions that you have about the topic—leaving artifacts behind for the next group that visits your table.
   c. Your teacher will call time after four or five minutes, and each of you will move to another table.

continued

3. As you move to a second table group, try to be in a group with no more than two or three students who were in your first group. The idea is to dialogue with the maximum number of classmates over the course of the discussion time.

4. As the new round begins, follow the same protocol as in #1, with attention to the following.

   a. During each new round, the table host will summarize previous groups' thinking and allow time for the "new" group to read through the comments left behind by previous groups to stimulate your thinking.

   b. Be sure, during your group's discussion, to add your comments to the "tablecloth."

5. After four rounds of talk, return to your initial table.

   a. The table host/facilitator will lead the group in reviewing all the comments that were added.

   b. Finally, the table host will lead the group in talking about other insights gained during the process of table rounds.

Learning to Question

Discussion differs from recitation in many ways. An important cognitive skill that students must develop in order to engage in discussion is questioning. In traditional classrooms, in which recitation is the predominant form of questioning, teachers ask almost all the questions. Students learn this going-to-school behavior well: *Students answer questions; they do not ask them.* Yes, there are those few students who seem to ask questions all the time, but for the most part, the experience of school involves answering (not asking) questions. In fact, school observers rarely record students asking content-based questions. We challenge you to audiotape a class and count the number of teacher and student questions. Who asks more? We hope you don't fit the "pattern," but in many classrooms, student questions are a rarity.

Question asking is key to learning. It's part of the social, cognitive, and use-of-knowledge skills that support discussion. Because it's not a skill that students typically use or practice in school, the skill of asking questions might be the most difficult to teach. Asking a question requires true student engagement. When students ask questions about the content, show puzzlement, or wonder openly, we know they are thinking!

A key to helping students pose questions is to help them understand the difference between typical "school-type" questions and "true questions." Examples of school-type questions are clarification and procedural questions such as *What are we supposed to do?* and *How can you solve this problem without knowing the distance?* Such questions are necessary and routine, but they are not true questions. A true question is rooted in genuine curiosity.

Curiosity isn't featured in most questions students are used to hearing, or asking, at school. For example, if a teacher asks students to write questions based on a passage of text, a math problem, or artwork, students are likely to write questions like these: *What are the names of the planets? What is photosynthesis? What are the major colors in this picture? What triggered the Revolutionary War? Who was the main character in the book? What happened early in the movie (or book) that forecast what might happen later?* These are questions for which students probably already know the answers. Such questions check for understanding, but they don't display curiosity.

True questions pertain to things students wonder about or are puzzling over, for which they don't have the answer—or even *an* answer. Questions like these:

- I wonder if this story is partly autobiographical. Did the author have a lonely childhood? It seems like he understands very well what it must feel like to be poor and an orphan.
- What do you think motivated the Founding Fathers? I mean, they didn't want to pay taxes to England. But here we are, years later, paying taxes to our government. What's the difference?
- I don't understand why, when I multiply whole numbers, I get a bigger number. But when I multiply fractions, I get a smaller number. It seems like it's backwards—and that it should be division, not multiplication.

Notice that a question doesn't necessarily end with a question mark. But all of these "questions" are signs of student thinking—and of their desire to know more or to make sense of a seeming contradiction.

The four protocols we describe give students practice in formulating questions. They are presented here in order of decreasing need for teacher support. Once students have mastered the skill and questions come easily, the scaffolding built into these protocols can be used less frequently because questions will be a natural and valued part of the classroom.

See-Think-Wonder (STW)

One of the thinking routines in *Making Thinking Visible*, See-Think-Wonder, is a favorite for helping students learn to pose true questions (Ritchhart et al., 2011). It begins with the teacher presenting an image that every student can see clearly, allowing sufficient time (depending on the complexity of the image) for all to see it, and asking, "What do you see?" In the early grades, and in early uses with older students, this can be done as a whole class so that students get feedback to help them understand the difference between what they see and what they think about what they see. They can be encouraged to notice details that might not be mentioned initially. When doing this as a whole class, the teacher can record the ideas so all can see what has been said. After practice, students can work in small groups or record individually and share with a partner.

Second, the teacher asks students, "What does it make you think?" or "What do you think about what you see?" Here, speculations and interpretations are encouraged. As students respond, the teacher keeps them focused on the image by asking follow-up questions such as "What do you see that makes you say that?" and "Does this part of the image make you think of anything?" Finally, having surfaced the concrete and students' interpretations of it, the teacher asks, "What do you wonder about what you see?" or "What does it make you wonder?" A wondering is something they would like to know more about; wonderings should be connected to or prompted by the image.

After students learn the STW routine, they can work in self-managing groups of two, three, or four. Teachers might wish to create heterogeneous groups that include a variety of learning preferences (e.g., visual, auditory, and interpersonal) so that each group has different perspectives on what they see, think, and wonder.

See-Think-Wonder in Action

Contributed by Jennifer Oliver, 4th Grade Math Teacher
Paschal Elementary School, Schertz, Texas

I was about to teach a unit on decomposing fractions with like denominators. The "I can" statement of the related 4th grade math TEKS (Texas Essential Knowledge and Skills) reads as follows: **4.3 E: I can add and subtract fractions with equal denominators, using objects, pictures, number lines, and numerals.** I selected See-Think-Wonder (STW) as a strategy because I wanted to know what my students remembered about adding fractions, as represented on a number line. I also wanted to introduce STW as a tool my students could use to analyze the complex graphics now included in answers to word problems on the standardized math test. With practice, I hoped that students, having used STW with peers, would begin to automatically ask themselves, "What do I see?" "What do I think about what I see?" and "What do I wonder about what I see?"

The class had recently been on a field trip to a local garden, where they had lessons on square-foot gardening. They had made connections with the gardening to math and arrays. I introduced STW to my class by using a colorful photograph of a garden and asking them, as a group, "What do you see?" Responses included "a garden," "six square feet for gardening," "a trellis," "strings separating the squares," and so forth. Then I asked, "What do you think about what you see?" The students responded, "I think this person loves to garden because it's very well maintained" and "I think this could feed a family." For each statement, I asked the students to link back to the picture to provide evidence. Finally, I asked, "What do you wonder?" and gave a sample wondering. The students posed questions: "Are there other gardens near that one?" "I wonder if the person who dropped that spade took the picture?" "I wonder if it's a family that gardens there?"

continued

Now that the students had learned about STW, they were ready to apply it to math and talk to one another. The next day, I gave every class member a number line such as the one below. On the paper were three questions: "What do you see?" "What do you think about what you see?" and "What does it make you wonder?" I asked them individually to look at the picture and answer the three questions.

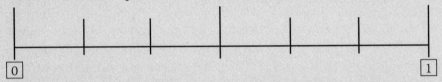

I then asked students to share their answers to the first question with a partner. I heard the following comments as partners talked: "I see a number line." "I see eight spaces on the number line." "I see a number line divided into eighths." "I see a halfway point." "I see seven lines between the numbers 1 and 0." "I see nine lines." After overhearing, "I see 1/8, 2/8, 3/8, 4/8, and so forth," I provided a prompt: "Do you see those numbers?" The student replied "No." I suggested, "OK, let's hold off on what you *think* about what you see and stick with what you *see* for right now. That's our next step."

I then asked students to share in their groups what they wrote in response to the question "What do you *think* about what you see?" Here are some comments I heard as I listened to the groups talk: "They're trying to see how many spaces there are between 0 and 1. Like the number lines on our math contract." "That the number line is divided into eighths." "Yeah, but there's only seven lines." "I think this has something to do with fractions." "I think somebody is trying to record data on a number line." "I think the number line has eight parts." "I think there will be more spaces after the 1." "Like Jeff, I think it's fractions." "I think it's unfinished because it's going to go past 1." "I think someone will fill it in; it looks empty with those lines." "I think the center line equals 1/2."

Next, I wanted them to pose questions. "What does this make you wonder? Go around your group and give one wondering from each person until all the questions in your group have been asked. The recorder should keep notes about the questions." As I walked around and listened, I heard the following: "I wonder if this is how I should have done my homework." "I wonder if numbers are going to fit on the number line." "Why are there only seven eighths and not eight eighths?" "I wonder if we can use this number line to add fractions." "I wonder if the numbers are fractions or multiplication problems." "I wonder what kind of fractions can go on the number line." "I wonder if it's going to be a decomposed fraction on a number line."

I told them, "You have lots of good questions—and several of you incorporated our learning target!" I paused and continued. "Let's take one of your wonderings and see if you can figure it out with your home group: 'I wonder if fractions are going to go on the number line.' As a group, talk about this. Speculate. Remember to give evidence for your thinking."

The classroom exploded in a buzz of conversation at every table. Every group finished quickly, as they had gotten the idea from hearing others talk that there were eight equal parts on the number line. I then asked about another wondering I'd heard: "Why are there only seven eighths and not eight eighths? Can you explain this in your groups? Be ready to share." Again, there was a buzz and students easily figured out this problem.

I closed the lesson by posing a question for students to solve in their groups: *I have a wondering, too. It's like something I heard as I walked around. I wonder how I can use this number line to prove this math sentence: 7/8 = 3/8 + 4/8?* Again, the class got it quickly and seemed to understand how to use a number line to add fractions.

As I reflected on this activity, I realized that this structure would be helpful in the future. I plan to use it multiple times so that my students can use it as a tool for their thinking about math word problems and graphically displayed response options. For the first-time use, I thought the structure helped my students voice some important questions—and they voiced some misconceptions that they were able to address with peers.

Think-Puzzle-Explore (TPE)

Another thinking routine popularized in *Making Thinking Visible* is Think-Puzzle-Explore (TPE) (Ritchhart et al., 2011). The verbs *wonder* and *puzzle* communicate the essence of questions that drive learning. The TPE routine is akin to KWL (What do you *know*? What do you *want* to know? What have you *learned*?), which is a traditional way for teachers to involve students at the beginning of a unit of study. Unfortunately, KWL often moves students to provide "the teacher's answers" to these questions. Students mention only the facts that they are fairly certain about and then try to guess what the teacher thinks will be important for them to learn. Rarely have we witnessed classrooms where "What do you want to know?" results in true questions or wonderings from students.

TPE is commonly used at the beginning of a lesson or unit to stimulate student interest, to formatively assess student knowledge and interests, and to identify misconceptions. Some teachers use this at other points in a unit to formatively assess student learning. The difference in the wording produces different results:

- "What do you *think* you know about [the given subject]?" Allow sufficient time for students to think about the question. They can write their responses and share with a small group, or respond as a large group, piggybacking on one another's ideas.
- "What questions or *puzzles* do you have about it?" You might model this for students the first time, using phrases such as "I wonder about _____" and "I am curious about _____" and "I would really like to know _____."
- "How can we *explore* the puzzles that you identified?" Finally, students can have some input into how they might study this new topic by thinking about ways they might resolve some of their puzzles. "Who has an idea about how we might learn more about Andrew's puzzle?"

IQ Pairs

IQ Pairs uses a simple paired structure in which questions are one of the expected outcomes (IQ=Insight/Question). For a reading, a quote, an experiment, a video, or a math problem, ask each pair of students to identify an insight (something they learned or an "aha" experience) and a question they have about the topic. Teachers can choose from a number of alternatives as they move pairs into discussion. A very simple procedure is to ask each pair to merge with another, where they first share their respective insights, pointing to the position in the text from which each insight emerged and elaborating on what it means. Then, each pair poses its question, talking about why this is a puzzle and how they might go about investigating it. Teachers can then move into whole-class sharing and discussion.

Questioning Circle

To encourage student-generated questions, a text-based protocol called the Questioning Circle can be very useful. As in several other protocols, every student reads a common text. This time, the outcome of the reading is to formulate two or three thought-provoking and true questions or wonderings stimulated by the reading. Following a protocol similar to Save the Last Word for Me, each four-member student group appoints a facilitator (to assure they follow the protocol) and a timekeeper (to prevent any one person from monopolizing the discussion). Within each group, only one person speaks at a time; back-and-forth discussion is discouraged. A volunteer introduces the location in the text from which his or her question stemmed so that others in the group can understand the context for the question. The volunteer reads the text and then poses his or her question. In turn, each member of the group addresses the question by (1) using and citing information from the text, and (2) making speculations and inferences based on prior knowledge and information in the reading. When each member of the group has addressed the question, the person who posed it shares his or her thoughts about the question—referring to previous comments as well as relevant parts of the text. A second student offers a question, and the group follows the protocol to consider this second question. Time permitting, all four students will offer one of their questions for group consideration.

Now that you have considered some productive small-group protocols, we invite you to think with us about when you might use each. By no means should the selection of a structure and related protocol be arbitrary; these strategies are not just one more way to "engage" students by talking. Rather, we suggest that thinking about the instructional purpose and students' developmental levels should guide teachers' decisions about which group structures to use when. Indeed, intentional planning for purposeful use of structured small-group discussion is key to its effectiveness. We turn next to addressing this important subject, using the five-stage process for discussion introduced in the previous chapter.

Planning for Productive Discussion through Small-Group Structures

The stages of the discussion process (see Figure 3.2 on page 80) have been modified to create an organizer for decisions and activities specific to structured small-group discussions (see Figure 4.4). This organizer is helpful when deciding how to structure small groups that will support students' "thinking together" about content while developing discussion skills.

Preparing

Preparation occurs before class and encompasses the following teacher tasks:

Analyze the learning targets. What will students be able to do if they achieve this target? Where are they in developing the requisite knowledge and skills? What is the next appropriate instructional step?

Target specific discussion skills. Where are students in the development and use of the social skills (speaking, listening, and collaborating)? What

Figure 4.4 | **Process for Planning Structured Small-Group Discussions**

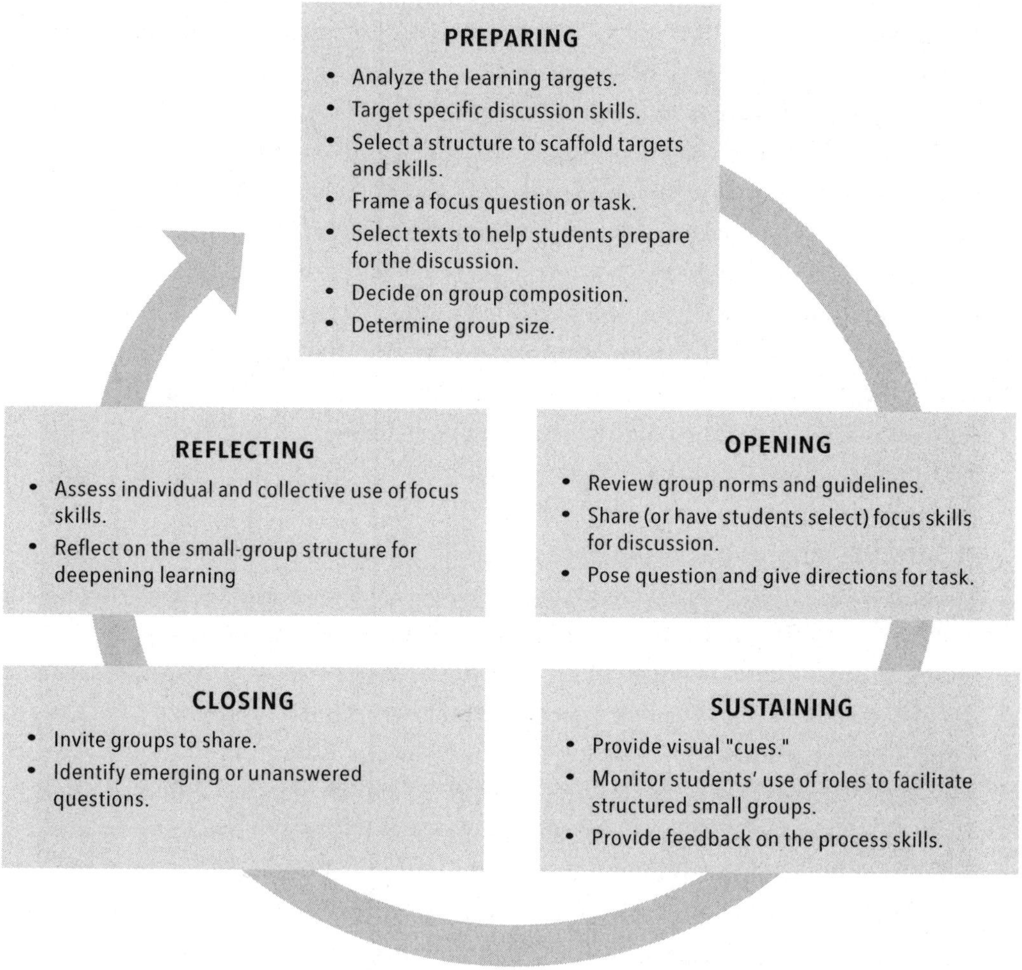

PREPARING
- Analyze the learning targets.
- Target specific discussion skills.
- Select a structure to scaffold targets and skills.
- Frame a focus question or task.
- Select texts to help students prepare for the discussion.
- Decide on group composition.
- Determine group size.

REFLECTING
- Assess individual and collective use of focus skills.
- Reflect on the small-group structure for deepening learning

OPENING
- Review group norms and guidelines.
- Share (or have students select) focus skills for discussion.
- Pose question and give directions for task.

CLOSING
- Invite groups to share.
- Identify emerging or unanswered questions.

SUSTAINING
- Provide visual "cues."
- Monitor students' use of roles to facilitate structured small groups.
- Provide feedback on the process skills.

cognitive skills do they need to learn and practice? What are two or three appropriate skill areas on which they could focus? Will the teacher select or recommend focus areas—or invite groups to select skill areas on which they want to focus? (See Appendix A for a comprehensive listing of skills for discussion.)

Select a structure to scaffold targets and skills. Choose one that is appropriate to where students are in the learning cycle. A caution: don't use group structures as ends in and of themselves to keep students busy and engaged. Be sure they are purposeful.

Frame a focus question or task. Frame a task or question around which students will engage in collaborative thinking and talking. This question should have no single correct answer and should take students beyond the basic memory level, requiring them to demonstrate understanding (summarizing, predicting, using evidence, etc.) and other higher-level thinking skills. It should also engage them in talking to one another, in pairs, or in small groups.

Select texts to help students prepare for the discussion. If the discussion question will be focused on text, the teacher needs to select appropriate text(s) for students. This reading can be done before or during class. The text should relate directly to the content standard or learning target and be engaging, thought-provoking, and challenging.

Decide on group composition. There is no magic bullet for this important decision; rather, it will depend on the selected protocol and on the students' comfort and experience in speaking with others. Many teachers establish "home groups" that stay together for four to six weeks so that students become comfortable working with one another; it takes less time to organize for a discussion when students are already part of a functioning group. Students can sometimes leave their home groups to work in "interest groups" such as Book Clubs or Literature Circles, and teachers might occasionally mix it up by having students number off to form random groups. For example, sometimes teachers will choose random groupings because the protocol (e.g., the Final Word) assures that everyone will contribute equitably. If the class is diverse in reading abilities, teachers may intentionally create heterogeneous groups to get a mix of ability and comprehension. At other times, grouping "talkers" together helps students learn how difficult it can be to get a word in when others are talking so much! Likewise, a group composed of "hesitant talkers" can demonstrate to members how important it is for everyone to speak if a group is to function well. (See the following story for an example of how one teacher formed discussion groups.)

Determine group size. The selected protocol will also influence group size. For example, if a teacher is using Ink Think in a class of 25 and has created five questions, each group would consist of five students, or one-fifth of the class. However, if the teacher wanted students to use this protocol to respond to three questions, he or she might create two groups for each question so as to keep the group size manageable.

Because pairs are extremely functional and are used frequently and for a wide range of purposes in most classrooms, many teachers begin by thoughtfully matching students to form effective twosomes. They then determine which pairs might work well together so they can quickly form quads when using text-based protocols or other protocols that require a greater number of students to produce more and more diverse responses.

A "Divide and Conquer" Strategy to Organize Small Groups

By Kim Sidorowicz, 7th Grade Humanities Teacher
Lower Manhattan Community Middle School, New York, New York

I was inspired to create groups for discussion that would work in my classroom setting after attending a workshop presented by Jackie and Beth. On my train ride home, I began by sketching a layout for my classroom. I continued through the evening to think about how best to establish groups. I teach two sections of 7th grade humanities in an ICT (Integrated Co-Teaching) setting. Each class has over 30 students with a variety of needs, personalities, and preferred learning styles. I had a lot to consider as I planned groups that would optimize talents and engage all students in thinking through discussion.

continued

After determining I would need seven groups of four and one group of five to accommodate the number of children in the class, I thought about the roles for groups that we had used in our workshop and decided to select students who would best serve in each of these roles. I clarified my thoughts about the students for each role (see Figure 4.5). First, I selected eight students who would serve as a Facilitator for each group. These students were leaders, confident enough to speak in groups, and good readers. Next I identified nine Time Keepers/Materials Managers (one group had two for these roles), a Questions/Sticky Notes Manager for each group, and Recorders.

Figure 4.5 | Desirable Traits for Students Assigned to Various Roles for Small-Group Discussions

Facilitator/ Reporter (Role #1)	Time Keeper/ Materials Manager (Role #2)	Questions/ Sticky Notes Manager (Role #3)	Recorder (Role #4)
• Viewed as positive leaders by peers • Patient • Encouraging • Articulate • Avid independent readers	• Need help with time management • Not confident sharing out in larger groups • Largely tactile learners • Read "only when asked/told" what to read, or do not read much outside of school for enjoyment	• Usually ask a lot of questions • On grade level in reading • Like to arrange items/ place things in order • Various comfort levels in group sharing	• Typically quiet in class but enjoy writing • Take great notes • On grade level in reading or slightly below grade level • Various comfort levels in sharing with classmates

I gathered the students together by roles, reviewed their role description, and practiced their job responsibilities. (See "Roles for Small-Group Discussions.") A special "hit" was that the Time Keepers were allowed to use the timer on their smartphones; other than that, phones were not allowed in my class. The Time Keepers especially loved the fact that they could set the timer to their own chime! Time is of the essence in a classroom, so my Time Keepers feel especially important. The Facilitators keep the small discussion groups running like well-oiled machines. They repeat directions as needed, further explain a set of instructions in "kid-friendly" language, and cheerlead the group to success by keeping the group on task and on topic. My Questions/Sticky Notes Managers write questions from the group members on the sticky notes. If it is a question requiring an immediate answer, they raise the sticky note to indicate teacher assistance is needed. Otherwise, the sticky notes are placed in the group folders for us to answer at a later time. Recorders keep track of the conversation flow, record in-the-moment discussion notes, and report back to the Facilitator.

Roles for Small-Group Discussions
7th Grade Humanities
Sidorowicz/Sinclair

#1. Group Facilitator/Reporter
- Keeps group members on task/topic
- Starts off the discussion and helps bring the discussion to a close
- Checks in with *every* group member to make sure *all* voices in the group are heard
- Reports the small-group discoveries to the larger group

#2. Time Keeper/Materials Manager
- Assists with time management
- Provides a time for each group member to speak
- Organizes/distributes all materials used and returns the materials to the proper place (includes laptops, pens, paper, etc.)
- Collects work and puts the work in the proper folder or grading basket

#3. Questions/Sticky Notes Manager
- Writes any questions the group may have on a sticky note
- Signals teacher when clarification for the group or an individual is needed
- Reviews all directions and restates as needed
- Fills out the Group Rating Report Overview at the end of the month

#4. Recorder
- Documents the small-group responses in the format required for the group activity (e.g., on chart paper)
- Takes notes as needed
- Shares what the group discovers with the Facilitator/Reporter

Subs: If a member of the group is absent, subs will be needed. Ms. Sidorowicz and Ms. Sinclair will appoint subs as needed.

---

continued

For ease of management and direction giving, I assigned each group a "direction" (N, S, E, W, NE, NW, SE, SW). Letters of the alphabet, names of animals, or colors would also work. Each role was assigned a number, as in the preceding description. Since I frequently differentiate by assigning readings that vary by reading ability, I can differentiate by distributing readings labeled #1, #2, etc. In addition, if I want students to talk in pairs outside of their home groups, I can ask the NW and SW tables to partner by numbers (1–4).

I let students know that we would assess the groups after a month of working together. Over the course of this first month, I have learned many new things about my students, and they have learned new strategies from one another. For one, the level of trust and respect is high; not one Time Keeper has attempted to use any feature on their phone other than the timer. Students who had low work production have increased their output by more than 90 percent. They feel accountable to their groups; the Facilitators' encouragement has gone a long way to build confidence so all students are sharing their ideas. We have seen time management and organization improve in our first month of this group organization. My co-teacher and I agree that our students have gained confidence, responsibility, acceptance, patience, and diligence. Students met in role groups to reflect on their success; all students completed an anonymous reflection about the success of their groups. The vast majority of students liked the current groupings and felt they were able to talk to peers they had previously not worked with on a consistent basis.

Interestingly, when students work in other groups (in Literature Circles, for example, which they self-select) they want to use the roles that we introduced. So other children get to try out being Facilitators, Time Keepers, etc.

I am thrilled with the results of our initial use of this organization for small-group discussions. I love to hear the voices of quiet students who now have gained confidence and find value in sharing their thoughts and ideas in their small group, which is ultimately shared with the large group. I believe this approach has provided a stronger voice for those students who typically remained quiet. For those with a more dominant personality, it has caused them to become more aware of their responsibility to share time to speak. The introduction of these discussion groups has enhanced our overall classroom culture.

Opening

The process for deciding on the best way to open a structured small-group discussion is similar to that used for a teacher-guided discussion.

Review group norms and ground rules. Teachers (or students, in their small groups) review the norms and ground rules for small-group discussion. In classes where small-group collaboration is standard, this review will be quick; if students are new to learning these ways of learning together, more time will be necessary. Begin by introducing a small number of ground rules, and keep the same ones for several weeks, until they become an accepted way of interacting. Eventually, students can develop their own ground rules; two nonnegotiables are equity in responding and speaking, and silence to honor thinking and reflection. When students develop the ground rules, they own them and will likely self-monitor and self-correct.

Example of Ground Rules for Structured Small-Group Discussions

Note that these ground rules encompass the three categories of norms described in Chapter 1: those related to the purposes of questions, think times, and participation.

continued

For Primary and Elementary School

1. Listen carefully to other students.
2. Ask questions if you don't understand what someone else says.
3. Learn from one another.
4. Be sure everyone contributes.
5. Allow time to think—before and after someone speaks.
6. Ask questions when you are curious.

For Secondary School

1. Be open to and respect all points of view.
2. Listen with an open mind and expect to learn from one another.
3. Accept responsibility for active and equitable participation by each group member.
4. Check for understanding. Before you counter an idea, be sure you fully understand what has been said.
5. Allow think time—before and after a group member speaks.
6. Ask questions.

Share (or have students select) focus skills for discussion. Teachers may suggest two or three discussion skills to target during a small-group protocol. Calling attention to the skills that a specific structure scaffolds will help students be mindful of these skills when they discuss without the assistance of a protocol. The teacher might ask students to consider what is most important to them, share their thinking within their small groups, report out to the full class, and collectively select two or three skills on which to focus. Recently, while visiting a classroom, we heard the teacher say the following as she introduced the topic for discussion: "Now remember. Today we want to be sure that everybody contributes, that we all have enough time for thinking, and that we build on what others say." This reminder helped the small groups pay special attention to these skills, and the teacher could provide guided practice for individual groups as she monitored.

Pose question and give directions for task. If the protocol to be used is new to the class, the teacher will need to explain the process in some detail; otherwise, the question (and directions) should be posted, with the teacher adding verbal instructions and reminders as needed.

Sustaining

The structure of small-group settings helps to sustain thinking as students become accustomed to following the steps or routines inherent in protocols. Also, because the teacher cannot be present at all times with all groups, students must assume responsibility for sustaining one another's thinking and speaking. The role of the teacher is to (1) intentionally model desired behaviors during direct instruction and teacher-guided discussion, (2) remind students of what skillful use of group processes looks and sounds like, and (3) provide support while "listening in" and monitoring student participation and conversation.

Provide visual "cues." Teachers may want to provide cue cards or post sample stems related to targeted discussion skills. The cards can provide ideas on how to encourage deeper thinking (e.g., "Could you say more about that?" or "Can you give me an example?"), how to ask for evidence (e.g., "I hadn't thought of it that way. Can you tell me where you got that idea in the text?"), how to get behind a student's thinking (e.g., "What makes you say that?"), or how to disagree respectfully (e.g., "I am really interested in what you're saying. It's different from what I was thinking. I'd like to hear you say more about your ideas."). (See Figures 2.3, 2.4, and 3.4 on pages 42, 48, and 97, respectfully, for additional prompts and stems.)

Monitor students' use of roles to facilitate structured small groups. Every student should be actively engaged in following group ground rules and working toward a productive discussion. It helps if groups identify leaders to facilitate their work together. (See the suggested roles in the example from 7th grade teacher Kim Sidorowicz.) These various group roles can be rotated regularly—or the teacher may decide to maintain them for four to six weeks. If a class is new to small-group discussion, teachers may want to assign roles, using student strengths and skills. In one 4th grade class we observed, the teacher assigned three roles: facilitator, recorder, and reporter. She gave the role of facilitator to the quietest student in each group, knowing that student was capable, but not likely to speak unless required to as facilitator. Upon reflection, the teacher was pleased with the results: each facilitator stepped up to his or her leadership role, posed questions to the group, and seemed to gain confidence.

Provide feedback on process skills. As teachers monitor group participation and discussion, they can take note of student intentionality in use of the targeted skills areas and provide feedback. Following are some examples:

- "When I hear you asking a question, Carly, it lets me know that you are listening to your classmates and thinking about what they are saying. You are modeling important skills for discussion: questioning, listening, speaking, and thinking."
- "Your facilitator is very skilled in following the protocol. I haven't seen any instance where two of you spoke at the same time. How does it affect your learning to pause and speak only when it's your turn?"
- "Do you remember that we said we would look for evidence to back up opinions and that we would clarify by asking questions about someone's statement? Let's look together at a recent comment I overheard. When Rick said he thinks the recent killings in Charleston, South Carolina, were a result of racism, and that racism is rampant in this country, what do you think he means by that statement? What are the implications? Do you agree or disagree and why?"

Closing

Invite groups to share. After students have participated in a structured group discussion, they will be interested in summarizing their own thinking and sharing it—and in hearing from other groups about what they discussed. Here are three options for closing the discussion:

1. **Reports from small groups.** Hear a report from each group about key ideas, questions, and conclusions (depending on the assignment). These may be posted and reviewed during a gallery walk if students

have used a protocol such as Ink Think, Affinity Mapping, or Sentence-Phrase-Word. Alternatively, the group reporter may make an oral presentation to share key ideas, questions, and conclusions. (See the sample template that follows for recording similarities and differences.)

2. **Fishbowl.** Conduct a fishbowl, composed of at least one representative from each group. Half of the classmates in the outside group will listen to and identify ideas that are similar to and different from ideas discussed by their small group. The other half will listen and watch for evidence of the targeted discussion skills and answer the following questions: "What is the evidence that we understand and can use our target discussion skills? What is the evidence that we might need continued work and practice with feedback?"

3. **Whole-group question.** Pose a question to the large group and hear from individuals, thus ending with what might be a teacher-guided or a student-led discussion, depending on the readiness and skill level of students as well as the instructional purpose.

Template for Recording Ideas from Small-Group Sharing

As you listen to group reports (during Fishbowl or group reports), use this template to identify patterns. In the first column, record ideas similar to those your group discussed or created; in the second column, record ideas your group did not generate or discuss; and in the third column, record interesting ideas you would like to hear more about or discuss further. Be prepared to share your notes with others in your home team to draw conclusions.

Ideas Similar to Ours	Ideas Different from Ours	Interesting Ideas to Learn More About or Discuss Further

Identify emerging or unanswered questions. However the closing and sharing are conducted, be alert for lingering questions related to the learning target. Ask individuals to record them on an exit pass or ask groups to generate questions on sticky notes to turn in for the next day's work.

Reflecting

At the conclusion of a structured small-group discussion, teachers can pose questions to help students assess and reflect on the discussion:

Assess individual and collective use of focus skills. It is helpful to ask students occasionally to assess their individual and group performance related to targeted skills and to submit these assessments in writing. (See Figure 3.4 on page 97.) When sharing out with the large group, the teacher or a student can record students' "big ideas" so the entire class can see (1) what about the process was engaging and helpful to understanding, and (2) what got in the way of learning. Alternatively, the teacher can engage the class as a whole in a discussion focusing on this issue.

Reflect on the small-group structure for deepening learning. Ask students to reflect on the experience of working in the selected small-group structure to deepen their understanding of content. This metacognitive task will help them be more aware of the value of working with others to learn; it may also help them be aware of their own preferences for learning, which may or may not have been used in the structure. As students begin to take charge of their own learning, teachers like to ask a question such as "How would you recommend we change or alter the process the next time?" They are often pleasantly surprised by student insights about how to adapt a process to better meet their learning preferences. Finally, as a formative assessment of the learning, ask students to complete an exit pass: "In what ways did you progress toward our daily learning targets as a result of your interaction with group members?"

A Final Word About Structured Small-Group Discussions

Small-group structures can be useful for attaining content-related targets. They engage students actively in making meaning and stretching their understanding—in ways that teacher presentations rarely can do. In addition, these structures scaffold many of the social, cognitive, and use-of-knowledge skills (and supportive dispositions) so important to effective discussion.

Persistent and strategic use of selected protocols brings to life the classroom culture associated with quality questioning and thoughtful discussions. For example, as students respond to an open-ended question via Think-Pair-Share, they are not trying to give the teacher "one right answer." Students speak freely to a classmate about the topic of the question; they don't expect or receive an evaluation of their response. The discourse is more natural than in most classroom questioning exchanges because a teacher evaluation does not follow each student comment. Rather, students talk together, sharing ideas and their own points of view, providing justification for their statements, listening to one another, and comparing others' ideas to their own. This simple structure begins to establish a different way of talking in the classroom—one in which students speak to one another (not just to the teacher), are individually accountable for responding, are thoughtful about what they say (instead of anxious to search out the "teacher's answer"), and are respectful in listening to understand a partner's response during a discussion.

Organizing students into small groups does not magically result in a transformed culture, improved discussion skills, or enhanced learning. If teachers and students are to reap the multiple benefits associated with structured small-group discussion, teachers must commit to systematic planning, using a process similar to the one presented in this chapter. When teachers begin with the ends in mind as they select protocols and make decisions about other structural elements, they increase the likelihood that powerful student learning will occur in these collaborative settings. Further, they are providing opportunities for students to assume increased responsibility for learning with and from one another through the use of disciplined discussion.

Reflecting and Connecting

Look back over the five categories of structured small-group discussions. Select one protocol from each category that you believe is appropriate for your students' age and developmental level and the content that you teach.

How would you introduce each identified structure to your students to be sure that they understand the discussion skills the structure scaffolds?

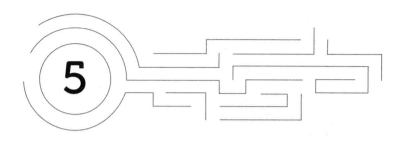

Student-Driven Discussion: Putting Students in the Driver's Seat

---

How can we support students in assuming responsibility to engage fully and thoughtfully in discussions?

In Ms. Pugh's 11th grade AP English class (Oak Mountain High School, AL), the students gathered in two concentric circles to discuss the book they had completed reading, *Big Fish* by Daniel Wallace. The inside circle discussed as the outside circle listened; then they switched places, giving both groups an opportunity to discuss. Two empty chairs in the inside circle allowed an occasional student from the outer circle to enter briefly to make a comment or ask a question. Students had prepared for the discussion by selecting a quote from the book that related to one of the issues they would discuss: mythology and the relationship between the two main characters, a father (Edward) and son (William). Each student also brought at least one open-ended question.

Ms. Pugh began the discussion with the following questions: *Mythical heroes usually undertake a quest for an object or some knowledge. What is Edward's quest? Does William have a quest?* Then she moved into the outer circle to monitor and provide support, if needed. Let's listen in on the students' opening remarks:

Student #1: My quote was related to the question. I thought Edward's quest was to put the virtues he had listed as important on page 122 of the book into his son. William [the son] says, "He made a list of the virtues he possessed and wanted to pass on to me: perseverance, ambition, personality, optimism, strength, intelligence, imagination. . . . Suddenly he saw what a great chance this was—how my empty-handed arrival was actually a blessing. Looking into my eyes he saw a great emptiness, a desire to be filled. And this would be his job as a father: to fill me up."

Student #2: I think William's quest was to get knowledge of his father. His quest was to get closer to his father, obviously, because on his deathbed he continually asked him questions. "You're my father and I don't even know who you are besides your myths." So I think throughout the whole book his quest was to have a relationship with his father.

Student #3: Do you think there's any significance as to why Edward always tells stories instead of giving William straight answers?

Student #4: He probably can't. [pause] I guess he doesn't have a bond with his son. He's gone all the time. He's never there. So maybe it was his way of trying to talk to him, but it was awkward. And the stories kind of made it even more awkward.

Student #5: Kind of like a defense mechanism.

Student #3: Was he trying to bond or was he trying to stay separate?

[After a bit more conversation, a student from the outer circle took an empty chair to pose a question.]

Student #6: One of the things I remember from the book is they say a big fish gets to be big by not getting caught. Well, were his stories a way of not getting caught? Or do you think William was trying to catch him?

Students responded with enthusiasm. "Good question!" said several students; they sat up straighter and seemed to have more energy; all were stimulated to think about the question. They thoughtfully continued to discuss the relationship between the father and son. Did the stories serve to bring them together or separate them? Did the father intentionally try to keep them apart? Or was he looking for a way to bring them together? The discussion yielded insights into the story—and into their own lives—that would have been unlikely if they read the book alone, not engaging in discussion to learn from one another.

The students in this class, with guidance from their teacher, had learned to assume responsibility for their own discussions. Ms. Pugh established the time, selected the text, and the organization (inside-outside circles) for their discussion. She asked them to prepare by bringing a quotation and a question from the book. She planned and posed the initial question, but then, unlike teacher-guided discussion, she moved into the outer circle, intervening only once with a reference to the class's Skype with the author. Students spoke as moved to speak, connecting with a prior comment, asking questions, and sharing their thoughts about the questions posed. Frequently, they referred back to a specific passage in the text. Ms. Pugh's goal was for her students to deepen their understanding of the text and its relationship to myths. She didn't have a specific outcome in mind; she didn't try to guide their thinking to a given conclusion. During the discussion, students stayed on topic, listened to one another, and expressed their own thoughts, learning from one another.

What Are Student-Driven Discussions?

Student-driven discussions are one way that students learn to accept increased responsibility for their learning. As suggested by the name, in this form of discussion, students are in the driver's seat. Teachers take a passenger seat, where they can monitor but not control. Students move the discussion forward by asking questions; making comments they can support with textual evidence; listening carefully to classmates' comments; and building on, agreeing, or disagreeing with others' remarks. They intentionally apply skills modeled by their teacher during teacher-guided discussions and reinforced through participation in structured small-group discussions.

Strategies for student-driven discussion go by different names, but they have important things in common. As Figure 5.1 shows, most are grounded in text or other material related to a topic under study. The "text" can be a passage (or, less frequently, an entire book) from literature, science, history, or health; a math problem that can be solved using multiple approaches; a video segment; artwork; words from a song; or a musical recording. The discussion usually begins with a teacher's question and is sustained by students. The teacher often sits outside the circle, seldom interjecting his or her voice into the conversation. The goal for the discussion is not to reach a decision, agreement, or consensus on a topic, but rather to move toward collective understanding—that is, a deeper understanding of how all students think and why.

Throughout the dialogue, students make their thinking visible as they give evidence for their ideas and reasons to support their thinking. Students engage in higher-level thinking during discussions as they analyze, evaluate, and think of new ways to put ideas together creatively. As with other forms of discussion, students are aware of the skills that contribute to effective discussion and, for each discussion, select one or more goals for themselves related to the social, cognitive, and use-of-knowledge skills introduced in Chapter 2.

Socratic Circles: Recommended Reading

High school teacher Matt Copeland (2005) writes compellingly of how the use of discussion in his English classrooms positively impacts student engagement and levels of thinking and discourse. Copeland adapted the Socratic Seminar to what he calls Socratic Circles, an inside-outside circle approach, with the inside circle composed of participants and the outside circle composed of observers who listen and offer feedback and then replace the inside circle to discuss. He gives practical suggestions for preparing for, facilitating, and assessing the process of his two-circle discussions. This is a helpful book for any teacher who wants to wade into the waters of student-driven discussion. Teachers of all grade levels and subjects can adapt Copeland's methods for their students.

Copeland, M. (2005). *Socratic circles: Fostering critical and creative thinking in middle and high school.* Portland, ME: Stenhouse.

Figure 5.1 | **Types of Student-Driven Discussions**

Type of Discussion and Source	Role of Facilitator/Teacher	Preparation by Students Before Discussion	Time and Grouping	Role of Students in Outside Circle
Shared Inquiry Based on the work of Robert Hutchins and Mortimer Adler, this discussion strategy was developed by the Great Books Foundation. The handbook for the process is available online: http://www.greatbooks.org/wp-content/uploads/2014/12/Shared-Inquiry-Handbook.pdf	• Selects text • Actively questions throughout discussion; does not offer own opinions • Sits with students in the circle • Questions to get behind the thinking of speakers, asks for evidence from text, solicits opinions from other students	Read text twice; mark interesting passages; if nonfiction, identify author's main ideas and how each is supported; bring interpretive questions that challenge their understanding of the text	40–120 minutes One group in a circle	n/a
Paideia Seminar Based on Adler's work, this strategy fosters critical and creative thinking through seminar dialogue, intellectual coaching and mastery of information. http://www.paideia.org/	• Selects text • Prepares and asks openended questions • Participates in discussion (although some teachers refrain from this role) • Takes notes about content and process	Read text twice to identify main ideas, questions, unknown words; select one or more goals for the discussion	90–120 minutes One group of 20–25 students in a circle	n/a
Socratic Seminars A process of dialogue based on Paideia and Great Books (Mortimer Adler et al.). Video description available: http://socraticseminars.com/socratic-seminars/	• Reviews ground rules for discussion • Selects text • Prepares three to five questions • Begins by asking openended question • Facilitates and participates actively in discussion (*Note:* The degree of teacher involvement in the discussion varies from teacher to teacher.)	Read selected text twice, analyzing for meaning; identify main ideas and questions	20–45 minutes One large circle or inside-outside circles	Options: Each student may: • observe one student, preparing to give feedback; • track the whole group; • listen and think about own ideas related to others'.

continued

Figure 5.1 | **Types of Student-Driven Discussions** (*continued*)

Type of Discussion and Source	Role of Facilitator/Teacher	Preparation by Students Before Discussion	Time and Grouping	Role of Students in Outside Circle
Socratic Circles This strategy, a variation of the Socratic Seminar, is described as used by teacher Matt Copeland in his 2005 book *Socratic Circles: Fostering Critical and Creative Thinking in Middle and High School*. Note: Some teachers use the term *Socratic Circles* to refer to other variations of student-driven discussions.	• Identifies text(s) related to standards under study • Prepares three to five questions and possible follow-up questions that might be appropriate • Poses one question • Steps outside the group to observe; does not actively discuss • Enters group only when necessary	Read text twice; annotate per suggestions by teacher to identify questions, main ideas, unknown vocabulary words, etc.	Inside-outside circles (randomly formed and changed weekly). Inside circle is seated on the floor; outside on chairs. Weekly. Each group discusses for 10 minutes, with feedback after both groups.	Listen and give specific and descriptive feedback to the observed discussion. Some have specific tasks: to track big ideas; to track who speaks; to track specific use of language in goal areas.
21st Century Fishbowl Developed by Amber Pope, teacher, Tarrant High School, and Beth Sanders, Technology Integration Specialist, Tarrant (AL) City Schools	• Identifies topic for discussion • Provides assignment to students for preparation • Prepares and poses opening question • Monitors inside circle discussion • Participates in outer circle's tweets	Prepare per teacher assignment	Each group discusses for 15–20 minutes.	Listen to discussion and tweet their own ideas, questions, and additions to one another and to the public about comments, preparing to move to inside circle

Roundtable Developed by Cheryl Olcott, teacher of communications, Parkersburg South High School (WV).	• Provides a number of topics from which students select every week • Reads the papers and articles from students • Prepares questions; asks or comments only rarely • Sits in circle, takes notes of conversation, indicates the order of upcoming (volunteer) speakers • Names a Roundtable student leader	Write a one-page essay about the selected topic; identify and print off an article that backs up his point of view, attaching a source page, to help learn how to provide evidence that backs up opinions. In addition, students are encouraged to bring a quote (related to the topic) and one or more questions.	60–90 minutes weekly One large classroom group (20–35)	n/a
Literature Circles or Literary Circles Described in various books and Internet sites	• Might recommend books from which students can choose • May name a facilitator and recorder for every group, to ensure groups stay on topic—eventually allows students to self-select these roles • May prepare questions that students can use if the group stalls	Read a passage, chapter, or entire book carefully and think about what they would like to discuss; debrief the discussion process and summarize what they learned.	10–25 minutes Students join small groups (3–8) based on preferred reading	n/a

The Changed Roles of Teachers and Students

Just as there is no "one right answer" in a true discussion, there is no "one right way" to conduct a student-driven discussion. Teacher choice, based on the desired learning outcomes and the readiness of both students and the teacher, will dictate the type and format of the discussion. Play with it. Try out different styles. Select and adapt a discussion method that works for you, your students, and the time you have available. Stick with it so that students learn how best to participate over time. Student-driven discussions will likely be a weekly or bi-monthly event, one that students will eagerly anticipate. Too many changes in the format or the rules will be confusing and may weaken the strength of this approach.

The one constant is that students assume more responsibility for their learning by becoming responsible partners with other students in exploring and making meaning together. Does this mean teachers give up all control and responsibility? Absolutely not! However, the teacher's role shifts from a "typical" teacher role, as he or she isn't dispensing information, giving directions, or actively participating in the discussion. Rather, the teacher steps back after posing an initial question, assuming the roles of *supporter* and *monitor*. The teacher may literally "step back" out of the circle. This physical movement serves two important functions. First, it reminds students of their responsibilities to speak to one another (not to the teacher), to keep the discussion alive by asking questions that spring from curiosity, to identify connections between two or more ideas, and to use evidence to support their own comments. Stepping outside the circle also reminds the teacher to refrain from interjecting ideas or questions except as necessary.

After helping the discussion get off to a good start, as a *supporter* of the discussion, the teacher helps students understand their roles in discussions and as learning-leaders of the group. Only when necessary—that is, when students don't fill these roles—does the teacher intervene to keep the discussion on target, clarify incorrect information or facts, and move the conversation along if it gets bogged down.

As a *monitor*, the teacher may establish goals for the discussion (related to the social, cognitive, or use-of-knowledge skills identified in Chapter 2) or ask students to select individual goals. The teacher (and students in the outside circle, if there is one) keeps a running record of student progress toward those goals, noting specific examples of each. Throughout the discussion, the teacher takes notes on the flow of the content and documents any misunderstandings. Sometimes, the teacher or a designated student-observer does this on a whiteboard or easel paper. If a student makes a factually incorrect statement, the teacher waits to see if another student corrects the statement; if not, the teacher comes into the group to clarify the speaker's meaning. In so doing, the teacher dignifies the student's remark and explicitly notes his or her reason for entering the discussion—to model ways to ask a student to rethink what he or she said so that students can assume the role of "corrective feedback giver."

So how do we, as teachers, encourage our students to accept such responsibility? First, we have to give it up. Once we've laid the groundwork for a productive discussion (e.g., established ground rules, modeled and practiced appropriate discussion skills, and prepared a focus question that addresses the desired skills and standards), we have to let go of control of the conversation. The fact that we think we have control, when we are sitting in the group as a participant, is a bit of a misconception anyway. We don't control what students are thinking or what they might say. So loosen up the reins; move over and let the kids drive. Second, in the experience of teachers who have adopted this method, their students really enjoy being responsible! Discussion can engage students' thinking: they love to talk, and they like knowing that they are responsible for others' learning. They don't have the opportunity all that often, because during many classes, teachers do the thinking for them. But, when teachers are patient with the process, they typically find that students love these discussions and don't want to miss them.

Roundtable discussions are a regular feature in Cheryl Olcott's Communications class at Parkersburg South High School (WV). She recently asked her students, "What is the value of the roundtable discussions we have every week?" We include some of their responses to demonstrate how much students appreciate these opportunities for taking charge of their own learning:

- "In discussion we get to hear different ways of thinking about an idea."
- "It helps me to get information from others and to see how others see the world; it helps me in my perspective about life."
- "It helps us learn how to keep an open mind; we see different ways of thinking. When you're discussing, your values come into play—and some of us have different values because we have different backgrounds."
- "Discussion really challenges our thinking."
- "Not everybody has the same opinion. I love it. It's my favorite part of school all week! You get to talk and listen to others. And you have to think!"
- "Ms. Olcott uses what we say to ask deeper questions; those questions help broaden our thinking. But usually she doesn't say much. She tells us it's our discussion."

What does it mean to be responsible for your own learning? Most students have never really thought about it. The four-item survey in Figure 5.2, adapted from the writing of consultant Peter Block (2011), is one way teachers can ask students to reflect on what they bring to a learning situation and, in particular, student-driven discussions. Teachers have modified it for primary learners by simplifying the language, reading the items aloud, and using sticky notes to post opinions (represented by a smiley face, neutral face, or frowny face).

As teachers prepare students to lead their own discussions, they need to remind students: true discussion is not a "gab session" or a sharing of undocumented opinions. It requires careful and deliberate planning and preparation. Teachers play a prominent role in planning; however, students also have important responsibilities. Following are the roles of students and teachers throughout the five stages of the discussion cycle for student-driven discussion.

Preparing for Student-Driven Discussion

Preparing for discussion requires the teacher to take the lead on the four tasks described in Figure 5.3.

Figure 5.2 | Survey for Student Responsibility for Participating and Learning

Directions: Respond *honestly* to each of the questions by circling a number between 1 and 7. There is no "right" or expected answer. You should take into account your emotional, physical, and intellectual energy for today's discussion.

1. How valuable an experience do you plan to have during today's discussion—not what kind of experience do you want, but what kind do you plan to have?

1	2	3	4	5	6	7
Not valuable						Very valuable

2. How engaged and active do you plan to be?

1	2	3	4	5	6	7
Not engaged						Very engaged and active

3. How much risk are you willing to take?

1	2	3	4	5	6	7
Not willing to take risks						Very willing to take risks

4. How invested are you in the quality of the experience of other students? What is your level of concern about the well-being of your discussion group?

1	2	3	4	5	6	7
Unconcerned about others' learning						Very concerned about others' learning

Source: Adapted from content found in *Flawless Consulting*, by P. Block, 2011, San Francisco: Jossey-Bass.

Select Text

The teacher has a ready understanding of the learning targets and areas in which student understanding can be deepened and can use this knowledge to select a reading that will help prepare students for discussion. For example, if 3rd graders are learning to (1) recognize the relative movement of the Earth and moon in relation to the sun and (2) describe the similarities and differences among the planets, the teacher will select a reading related to the planets and their relationship to the sun. In fact, the teacher may select three different readings, to differentiate for student reading abilities; in all readings, the content will be similar. The teacher may find a science fiction reading, a thought-provoking poem or picture about planets, or a relevant image or video.

Figure 5.3 | **Tasks Associated with Preparing for Discussion**

Task	Teacher Responsibility	Student Responsibility
Select text	Choose a text that relates to the learning target(s), raises questions, and is relevant to students. The selection can be song lyrics, a poem, a short piece of fiction or nonfiction, a video clip, or artwork.	Sometimes suggest a song, text, or video that relates to the topic under study. (In Roundtable, students find Internet-based articles to support their thinking.)
Read text	Read the selection several times, looking for important literary devices, main ideas, potential questions, connections to students' experiences, potential misconceptions, and potential difficulties in reading or understanding.	Read teacher-selected text at least twice, looking for main ideas, questions, unfamiliar vocabulary, and interesting quotes. If reading a self-selected book, identify ideas and questions for potential discussion.
Frame focus question(s)	The teacher, if opening the discussion, will frame three to five questions as potential discussion starters—and will anticipate possible or likely student responses and plan for follow-up questions if not asked by students.	Bring questions to the discussion.
Determine organization for discussion and grouping of students	If there is to be an inner and outer circle, (1) plan how to assign students and (2) determine the role of the outside circle. If there are to be small groups (self-selected or teacher-assigned), select a facilitator until students can responsibly self-select.	If grouping by student choice, choose the book or topic you are interested in reading and exploring.

The Great Books Foundation (www.greatbooks.org) and the Touchstones Discussion Group (www.touchstones.org) are good resources for finding readings to stimulate discussions on whatever you may be studying. They also provide potential questions for discussion. Matt Copeland (2005) recommends *The Green Book of Songs by Subject: The Thematic Guide to Popular Music* (Green, 2002) and *Reading Teacher's Book of Lists* (Fry & Kress, 2006) as good resources for text.

What about students who are too young to read and discuss a passage of text for an extended period of time? Certainly even the youngest of students can discuss a book that has been read to them, with the teacher guiding the discussion; they can also participate in many types of structured small-group discussions. Primary grade teachers may introduce student-driven discussions in class meetings, perhaps once a week, during which students discuss how things are going in the classroom community. Teachers begin by asking students what went well this week, then move to things students would like to change or improve. In 1st to 3rd grade classrooms, teachers have reported a predominance of student talk (not teacher talk), with students successfully talking to one another, initiating questions, learning not to raise their hands to speak, solving problems together, pausing to think, and generally taking responsibility for productive discussions (Donoahue, 2001).

Read Text

Most text-based discussion strategies recommend that the teacher and students read the text at least twice. Often, teachers copy the text so students can freely write and annotate as they read. Teachers may suggest specific tasks for student preparation—for example, underline major ideas, write questions in the margin, circle words or ideas they are not certain about, and (for non-fiction) create an outline of major assertions and accompanying supportive statements. Teachers may ask students to turn in their annotations as a demonstration of their preparation.

Some teachers find it helpful to have the inner circle read the text aloud before beginning discussion, even when students have all read and studied it as homework. This allows everyone to hear the same words, with the same inflection. Touchstone advocates that all students read the text during class in order to level the playing field. Following their reading, students engage in preliminary small-group discussions to formulate questions and identify ideas of interest. Certainly, if students haven't prepared by reading, public reading will allow them some entry points into the discussion. With experience, students will understand that if they don't read and think about the text before class, they will not be able to engage as fully or understand as deeply as their peers.

If students don't prepare before class, a good strategy to help them get ready to discuss is showcased in a video from the Teaching Channel (2014) in which the teacher has students engage in an inquiry-based discussion of *To Kill a Mockingbird*. The teacher prepared a set of remember-level questions, which students responded to as homework. In class, students met in groups of four to share their responses. In this way, students all heard the correct basic facts of the text and were more able to participate in discussion about the text. Such practices establish an expectation of accountability among students to come to class prepared, as they know that others will be counting on their input to establish basic facts about the text.

Frame Focus Questions

A question for text-based discussion will emerge from the reading. For example, in the earlier science example about planets, the opening question might be this: *A foundation called Mars One is planning to establish a human settlement on Mars. What do you think they hope to learn?* If the students don't ask other questions, the teacher might prompt, "Let's assume an expedition travels to Mars. What would they need to take with them in order to live there, and why?" or "If Mars One is successful in sending a mission to Mars, would you want to go and live there? Why or why not?"

The teacher should formulate three to five questions that might work as an opening question for discussion. These questions, as mentioned earlier, should evoke several possible responses. They should be true questions that represent the teacher's curiosity and relate to students' experiences and interests. The questions should also be important to think about and should address an issue that students can truly understand only by hearing more than one point of view.

> "[Opening questions] should be questions that raise issues; questions that raise further questions when first answers are given to them; questions that can seldom be answered simply by Yes or No; hypothetical questions that present suppositions the implications or consequences of which are to be examined; questions that are complex and have many related parts, to be taken up in an orderly manner." (Adler, 1985, p. 175)

In addition to framing questions, teachers need to think about likely or possible student responses—including the dreaded situation of having no comments at all. Given sufficient think time, and no student comments, what might the teacher ask next? It might be as simple as pointing to the posted question and saying, "Turn to your partner and talk about this question." Or it might be a wondering: "I'm wondering why this question doesn't stimulate any comments. Does anyone have a comment they would venture to make?" Or it might be a check for student understanding of the question: "Would you restate this question in your own words?" [pause] "Jeremy?"

It's also possible that students will offer a response that is off-target or incorrect. In response to the Mars question, for example, some students might say, "They would want to take their pets, like their dogs and cats." Although the teacher hopes students will challenge one another's thinking when an answer is incorrect, especially during student-driven discussion, this doesn't always happen. If no student steps forward to correct a misconception or steer the conversation back on track, how should the teacher react? Preparation that includes anticipation of possible student responses helps teachers know when and how to step back into the circle. It's hard work and requires restraint for a teacher to know when to stay in the passenger seat and when to grab the steering wheel or apply the brake as the "driver's ed" instructor.

Students, too, need to have formulated questions before they enter the circle. One of the norms suggested in Chapter 1, "Ask questions when you are curious, perplexed, confused, or need clarification" is a good norm on which to focus if students are reluctant to ask true questions. Figure 3.4 in Chapter 3 suggests scaffolds that teachers can share with students to encourage their questions. Some of the structured group discussion formats suggested in Chapter 4 help students become more comfortable and skilled in posing questions. As mentioned earlier, this is one of the most difficult skills for students to master because it is so contrary to traditional "school" behaviors, where students are usually answering questions with a right answer—not asking them. Whether students have worked individually, with a partner, or in a small group to generate questions, they should bring some questions with them to the group discussion.

Too frequently, students "take turns" posing questions they bring into the circle—even if the question has no relationship to the prior comment or question. This kind of turn taking does not yield genuine dialogue. Imagine yourself discussing a problem with a colleague and saying, "I'm frustrated because Steven can read but doesn't seem to understand what he reads." How would you feel if your colleague responded with a question she had written the night before, such as "I wonder how the standards for algebra can be made relevant to 8th grade students?" Her question may be genuine, but it certainly doesn't send the message that she is listening to understand or valuing your question or comment. Likewise, students need help understanding that the questions they formulate before a discussion are simply prompts for thinking—not a script. They need to learn to ask questions that further thinking on the topic under discussion. There might be a time to pose a prepared question that takes the group to a new topic, but one must wait until the group is ready to move on. Meanwhile, the students' job is to identify new questions that arise as they listen carefully to others' comments. These more genuine questions are likely to bring energy and interest to the group—as in the chapter's opening vignette—and stimulate deeper thinking and consideration of the topic by all.

Determine Grouping

The teacher needs to decide whether students will discuss in one large group, in small groups around the room, in inside-outside circles, or in a fishbowl (in which one representative from each small group gathers in a central area to discuss, while classmates listen in and—when directed by the teacher or in some instances when they have something to add—replace the fishbowl member from their original group). Many teachers prefer inside-outside circles, as this format provides two major benefits:

1. Smaller groups (half the class) allow more students to speak and voice opinions.
2. When the discussing students (inside group) are aware of being observed both for the content and the process of discussion, they are more likely to be intentional about what they say and how they say it. The presence of an outside group doesn't impede open discussion; rather, it tends to increase the quality of the discussion.

For the inside-outside format, teachers need to assign students to one of the groups. Random selection (e.g., distributing two different stickers or numbered index cards to students on entry to class) is easiest; basically, what's needed is a cross-section of the class in each of the two groups. Self-selection by students is not recommended, as students will move to be in groups with their friends and this will influence who speaks during the discussion.

Typically, teachers allocate 10 minutes for preparation/organization/warm-up, 10 minutes for the first inside circle to discuss, 5 minutes for feedback from the outside circle, 10 minutes for the second inside circle to continue the discussion, and another 5 minutes for feedback from the outside circle. They might spend a final 5 minutes for individual or group reflection and the establishment of individual or group goals for the next discussion.

A priority for the teacher is to plan the task(s) of the outside circle. There are several options. The teacher may generate a list of discussion skills and assign some of them to each student, asking them to document examples and nonexamples of their assigned skills. Another option is to ask all students to listen to the discussion and track the main ideas as well as examples, text-based references or rationales, questions, and transitions. A third option is to assign each student in the outside circle one individual in the inside group on whom to focus, documenting examples of skills (e.g., asking another student for clarification, speaking clearly, making specific reference to the text, evidencing listening skills by building onto a classmate's comment, pausing to think before speaking, asking another student what she thinks). Finally, some teachers find value in assigning specific roles to selected members of the outside circle. In a video from the Teaching Channel that shows a Socratic Seminar in action (2013a), 11th grade English teacher Ms. Wu assigns one of the following roles to each of four students:

- Comment counter: Tracks how often each student in the inner circle speaks.
- Transition tracker: Records how the inner circle stays on topic as the students move from one student to another appropriately (e.g., summarizing what the student before had said, agreeing with a student, adding to a student comment).

- Quote tracker: Keeps track of specific references to the text.
- Discussion recorder: Graphically records the discussion on a whiteboard keeping track of the themes, questions, and examples of each theme.

Amber Pope, social studies teacher at Tarrant HS (AL), uses technology to engage students in the outside circle. As they listen to the inner circle discuss, they tweet their own thoughts, additions, and questions to others in the outside circle (see "Using Twitter to Engage Students During Discussion"). Students' engagement rates increase dramatically, as they actively listen and participate from the outside circle.

Using Twitter to Engage Students During Discussion

By Amber Pope, 9th grade social studies teacher, Tarrant High School, and Beth Sanders, Technology Integration Specialist, Tarrant City Schools, Alabama

At Tarrant High School, we believe students need multiple opportunities to practice and develop oral and written communication skills, engaging in critical and productive dialogue offline and online. Communication is no longer limited to face-to-face conversation; it's also happening virtually in a multitude of text, audio, and visual formats.

We support students as they develop their individual voices to explore their interests and passions, create and share content with an authentic audience, and practice and develop contemporary skills that will carry them into adulthood. Incorporating online discussion in the classroom is a game-changer. The use of social media is a powerful motivator to students. With proper facilitation of online discussion, students can develop and apply literacy skills using a platform with which they are comfortable and expert.

One method we have created to support development of student voice is the 21st Century Fishbowl, a new spin on a classic discussion method. In an inside-outside circle configuration, the inside circle discusses as usual. The outside circle tweets about what is said. The rest of the outside circle, the teacher, and others on Twitter can read the tweets in real time. The students stay engaged. When it's their turn to move into the inner circle, they are clear about what was said about the topic and are ready to continue the discussion verbally.

When we asked students, "In what ways did tweeting about the fishbowl discussion keep you engaged in learning?" they gave the following kinds of written responses:

- "It kept me engaged because it let me listen to what my classmates felt on the topic and how we agree or disagree."
- "It kept me engaged in learning because we had a big discussion about a topic and we all had our opinions; we kept it going and didn't get off topic. We asked questions and got really good answers from our peers."
- "I heard others' perspectives; that was engaging."
- "We were engaged because even though our voices were not being heard, we were still being heard on Twitter. We were still responding to the discussion by quoting and reflecting on our peers' thoughts."
- "It helped inform other people on what we're doing in class."

Online discussion provides immediate feedback to students: from other students, from the teacher, and self-assessment. "Favorite"-ing a tweet or retweeting it sends positive feedback to the student: they are on the right track and are saying something important. The teacher can also use this feedback to inform future instruction: What do students understand? Where do they have misconceptions or misunderstandings?

continued

We have found that Twitter is an excellent application for *public* online discussion. It helps with the following: becoming a responsible citizen in a digital world, building a professional network, creating a professional digital presence, using an economy of words, developing a point of view on important issues, interacting with diverse groups of people, viewing other people as resources, seeking feedback on ideas, and more. In addition, we believe that students improve their verbal expression of ideas as a result of online discussions. The internal processing required to formulate an idea into a coherent tweet transfers to live, face-to-face discussions. Reading others' ideas and responding to them translates into better listening skills.

With online discussions, equity is built in. All voices can be heard. All students can be simultaneously engaged. Students can carry on multiple powerful conversations at the same time. The natural consequence of creating this environment and allowing students this space is that they will be empowered to develop their voice and explore ways to use it.

If you want to learn more about this 21st century discussion format, use the QR code on this page to see directions given to the class, pictures of students discussing, and selected tweets.

https://storify.com/mssandersths/21st-century-fishbowl-popewildcat

For small-group discussions, the teacher may want to suggest the selection of a facilitator to ensure that all voices are heard and that the discussion stays on track. In the early stages of learning how to engage in this process, we recommend that the teacher select the facilitators. Some teachers select the most self-confident students, who tend to speak easily in the group. This leadership role prompts them to limit their own ideas, as they are responsible for seeing that others speak and share. Other teachers select students who are responsible but rarely speak in a group situation. As leaders, they have responsibility to speak in order to keep the group on task, posing questions and asking others to contribute. Once students fully understand what the role requires, they may move to group selection of their own facilitators, with the teacher monitoring and providing support as needed.

Opening: Activating Thinking and Setting the Stage for Discussion

Once students have actively read a passage, watched a video, or reviewed other selected materials—and have taken notes to prepare for discussion—the teacher needs to help "set the stage" for students to enter discussion, which is a different way of learning, thinking, and relating to one another. When students are old hands at discussion, they move into this state easily. But as they are learning to discuss—especially when they are assuming responsibility for student-driven discussion—they need to enter a "zone" for dialogue. Teachers ready students to discuss by attending to the tasks in Figure 5.4.

Review Class Norms and Ground Rules for Discussion

The considerations for readying students for student-driven discussion are similar to those related to teacher-guided discussion, described in Chapter 3. The teacher—or a designated student—reviews class norms and ground rules for discussion and encourages every student to take ownership of one or two ground rules on which to focus during the day's discussion.

Identify Focus Skills

The teacher facilitates students' intentional focus on discussion skills that will enhance individual or group performance. Sometimes, teachers present one to five skills for students to focus on during the discussion; at other times, each student might select and write (or circle) skills on which to focus. A compromise of these two approaches is probably best: teachers offer three to six goals, from which each student selects one to three. Thinking back to the most recent classroom discussion will guide teachers and students in the selection of focus skills.

Figure 5.4 | **Tasks Associated with Activating Thinking and Setting the Stage for Discussion**

Task	Teacher Responsibility	Student Responsibility
Review class norms and the ground rules for discussion.	May ask the facilitator to review discussion ground rules.	Read the ground rules and select one or more that merit special attention.
Identify focus skills.	Allow time for students to review skills and select those on which to focus as an individual or group.	Think together or individually about the skills on which to focus for improved discussion.
Activate student thinking.	Select a warm-up strategy, such as generating questions, identifying quotes in pairs, or sharing main ideas about the reading in small groups.	Engage fully in the warm-up activity.
Present the focus question for discussion.	Present the question (or designate a student to read the opening question).	If the teacher has designated group facilitators, they are ready to assume leadership to present the opening question.

Activate Student Thinking

To prepare students to engage in discussion, teachers find it helpful to activate student thinking by engaging them in silent, written reflection, Think-Pair-Share, or See-Think-Wonder in small groups. If the topic is likely to be polarizing, teachers may opt to begin with People-Graph (see Chapter 3) or Data on Display (see Chapter 4). Another good activator of thinking is Say It in a Word, in which teachers pose an opening question; allow time for students to write a reflection; and ask each student to summarize their response in a single word, going around the group to hear from each student. These strategies provide equitable opportunities for students to respond and to hear what others are thinking before they dive into the discussion. It also gives them something to ask others, such as "When you said 'difficult' as your one-word summary, what did you have in mind?"

The structure of the Roundtable, described in Figure 5.1, helps students learn and practice a variety of skills: integrating personal opinion backed by printed evidence; using persuasive techniques in the delivery of the message; listening, speaking, and viewing; and evaluating intrapersonal opinions in the framework of group communication.

On the day we observed Ms. Olcott's classroom, the discussion topic was "What does trust look like?" Every week since the beginning of school seven months earlier, Ms. Olcott's students had explored a topic together. The topics, like those recommended by McCann (2014), were essential for developing skills and dispositions associated with good citizenship; they included justice, responsibility, love, and others. The students were skilled at discussion; the excitement was palpable as all 30 students pulled their desks into a circle to think together about the question. To "warm them up" and ensure that every student made a contribution, the Roundtable began with each student saying something. Some chose to read their papers, while others posed a question, read a quote, or briefly shared their thinking about the topic.

The student leader began, "I think there are two different types of trust: you can trust others and you can trust yourself. My quote is, 'A bird doesn't trust the branch not to break, but trusts that he can fly away to safety if it does break.'" The student was holding a stack of shuffled index cards, each with the name of a student. After a brief pause, he called the name on the first card, moved it to the back of the pack, and continued until every student had responded. Following are some of the student responses from that opening:

- "For trust, I used the analogy of an eraser. It gets smaller and smaller after every mistake and eventually it's gone."
- "Trust is surrendering control."
- "Trust is like a broken mirror. You can't put it back together without seeing the damage."
- "I think deep down we all want to trust; we're just not sure how."
- "It's harder to trust if you've had a hard life."
- "Trust looks like a paratrooper jumping out of the plane. He has trust that his parachute will open and help him safely to the ground."

After everyone has contributed, the leader signals that they can move into more spontaneous conversation. Opening in this way appears to have two main benefits to the flow of the discussion. First, every student is accountable to share; those who don't like to speak in a group have the experience of doing it and may be encouraged to offer other comments. Second, every student is listening for connections—to his or her own ideas or among the ideas of class-mates—and has something on which to build as the discussion gets underway. When an opening piece, such as the previous example, offers such richness of thought from students, it is not surprising that the students can weave different ideas together to help formulate a more complete understanding of the idea of trust.

The first comment after the opening went something like this: "I would like to reflect on how Mackenzie, Laura, and Austin all referenced glass: like a mirror, a fragile vase, and [long pause, then other children prompt, "a piece of glass"] oh, yeah, a piece of glass. It's hard to put it back together once it crumbles." From this comment, students were moved to think about the relationship between trust and love, trust and respect, recovering from hurt resulting from broken trust, and differences between male and female expressions of emotions such as trust. Throughout the discussion, they posed questions, extended others' comments, speculated, and hypothesized.

As shown in a Teaching Channel video, "Socratic Seminar: Supporting Claims and Counterclaims" (2012), 10th grade English teacher Christina Procter helps students get ready to discuss by posing a set of questions to which students individually respond. They not only write what they think for each of the questions but also consider opposing responses they might hear from other students. Then they record how they might counter the claims made by peers who disagree. This gives students practice in thinking about what they themselves believe and what others might think and why. In groups of eight or so, they discuss the questions before beginning a fishbowl with representatives from each of the small groups.

Present the Focus Question

Most frequently, the discussion begins with a question prepared by the teacher. The question can be presented by the teacher or by a designated student. To encourage student responses, it should be presented with a bit of drama and prefaced with some context-setting, lead-in sentences. Most important, the teacher or student should pose the question in a way that communicates interest in what students are thinking and an expectation that great responses are forthcoming. This can be done through tone of voice, facial expression, and body language. As Adler phrases it, "Above all, the moderator must make sure that the questions he asks are listened to and understood, that they are not merely taken as signals for the person who is queried to respond by saying whatever is on his or her mind, whether or not it is a relevant answer to the question asked" (Adler, 1985, p. 175).

Sustaining the Discussion

In this stage, the three forms of discussion differ widely. In teacher-guided discussion, it is the teacher who primarily sustains the discussion through modeling, scaffolding, and coaching. As students participate in structured small-group discussions, the protocol itself scaffolds and sustains the discussion (with occasional teacher intervention). In student-driven discussion, the students themselves assume the major responsibility of keeping the discussion moving. Figure 5.5 depicts some major tasks of sustaining a student-driven discussion; most of the responsibility falls to students, with teachers ever ready to model and scaffold, if needed.

Students have a lot on their minds in a student-driven discussion: they must keep track of the flow of the conversation; listen intentionally to what is being said; remain mindful of their responsibility to voice opinions; monitor their performance in the skill areas on which they chose to focus; encourage others to contribute; and clarify their understanding of others' comments by asking questions, rephrasing, and so forth. Discussion engages students because it is rigorous and challenging.

Listen Thoughtfully

Mortimer Adler (1985), in *How to Speak, How to Listen,* asserts that listening for understanding is more difficult than reading to understand. Yet schools rarely spend time helping students learn to be good listeners. Adler points out that as we read, we can pause to think about what we just read, reread a passage that we didn't understand or that we tuned out on, or put the book aside to pick it up later.

Figure 5.5 | **Tasks Associated with Sustaining a Student-Driven Discussion**

Task	Teacher Responsibility	Student Responsibility
Listen thoughtfully.	Listen and keep a running record of the discussion.	Allow time for thinking and completing thoughts; take notes to keep track of the conversation.
Use think time to compare your thoughts to others'.	Monitor and remind students about think time, if necessary.	Think about others' comments: Do you agree? Disagree? Why? Help one another stay true to think times.
If unsure of meaning, ask questions to clarify.	Allow students to take on this responsibility; if they don't, intervene.	Decide if you are sure you understand completely what was said. If not, paraphrase to check or ask for clarification.
Once a comment is clarified, agree or disagree and say why; add to others' comments.	Refrain from expressing opinions.	Voice your agreement or disagreement and your reasons. Piggyback, add on, and give examples of what others have said.
Ask for evidence.	Allow students to take on this responsibility; if they don't, intervene.	Ask, "Where is the evidence? In the text? In another source?"
Ask questions about things that puzzle you.	Allow students to take on this responsibility; if they don't, pose a question.	Bring questions to the circle, but ask them only as appropriate to the flow of the discussion. Ask questions prompted by classmates' statements.
Correct mistakes of fact or misconceptions.	Allow students to take on this responsibility; if they don't, intervene.	Ask yourself, "Am I convinced of the factual truth of this statement?" If not, share your wondering and uncertainty.
Aim for equity in participation.	Keep a record of who speaks how often for use in reflection after the discussion.	Be aware that without all voices, the discussion suffers. Participate when you have something to say. Ask those who haven't contributed what they think.

However, "instant replay" is not an option when listening in a discussion. Once the words have been said, they are gone. Continual concentration is required to actively follow the speaker's line of reasoning. And yet, during a discussion, not only are we listening to the speaker, we are also listening meta-cognitively, to the questions that help us be active learners and participants: "What does he mean?" "Do I understand her point?" "Is that true?" "What is the evidence?" "Do I agree or disagree?" "How does this compare to what I was thinking?" At the same time, we may be formulating a response and wondering, "Should I voice this thought?" In other words, while we are listening to the speaker, we are also listening to many voices in our heads that can distract us from what is being said.

Adler (1985) suggests that students take notes during a discussion to help focus their listening. He acknowledges that some people consider it rude to write while listening to another instead of maintaining eye contact and giving other nonverbal signals that indicate one is listening. Adler contends, however, that since listening is so demanding, it requires note taking so that one can look back at what was said and reflect on it.

Use Think Time

An intentional silence between comments allows students time to think and process what has been said. It is especially hard to wait when the topic arouses strong feelings. But processing time is essential. It not only allows listeners to "step back" from their emotional responses, but it also allows them to ponder what was said, wonder what was meant, and wade through the many options for responding. When students are leading the discussion, they assume responsibility for helping one another remember to pause. They might do this by holding a "mini-discussion" after the main discussion to talk about signals they can use to remind one another to allow this silent thinking time. Or each speaker might agree to hold up a hand or otherwise signal for others to listen and not interrupt, keeping the hand raised for a few seconds after they finish. Or one member of the class (in the outside circle, or one who steps out of the large circle to monitor) may be asked to keep a running record of the amount of time between comments for feedback to students.

Sometimes in a discussion, the silence can seem prolonged. A teacher's natural impulse is to jump in to prevent students from getting uncomfortable with the silence and "save" them by making a comment, clarifying a question, or posing another question. However, we have learned the value of "waiting it out." Doing so requires a belief in the group: an understanding that although no one is moved to speak at that moment, as they use the silence to reflect, someone will offer a comment or question. Often, this silence transforms a discussion into a deeper, more reflective experience. One way to encourage productive silence is to acknowledge that a three- to five-second pause can seem awkward, and a 15- or 30-second pause may seem endless. Talk with students about the value of waiting and thinking. It is no one's responsibility to jump in to fill the void. Rather, encourage students to sink into the silence, replaying in their minds what was just said, and considering where they would like to move the discussion next. They should speak when they are ready—not because they feel the need to break the silence.

Ninth grade English teacher Paige Price shares an example of this long pause from her class's seventh Socratic Seminar. Her students are still learning the process, with guidance from the teacher, as shown in the Teaching Chan-nel video "Socratic Seminars: Patience and Practice" (2013b). Following the opening question, there is a long silence after Ms. Price withdraws from the Socratic Seminar and acts only as an outside facilitator. Commenting on this silence, she explains, "It's every teacher's nightmare to start a Socratic Seminar and have no one participate. To sit and wait and wait and wait. . . . But when we are telling students that it's their job to carry the conversation, we have to commit to that. . . . It's our responsibility to make it their responsibility."

If Unsure of Meaning, Ask Questions to Clarify

In classes where a teacher guides a discussion, actively modeling and scaffolding, students observe the teacher exemplify ways to ask for clarification. In student-driven discussion, it becomes the students' responsibility to decide when and how to do this. After a confusing or unclear contribution, the teacher should wait and see if students ask for clarification by saying something like "Could you say that another way?" "When you say that Mr. Arable was mean to Wilbur, what exactly do you have in mind?" or "Let me see if I understand what you just said. You think that Mark Twain was racist?" If no student seeks to clarify, and students begin agreeing or disagreeing without having clarity, the teacher might lean into the group and pose a question or rephrase the original statement to assure clarity.

Once a Comment Is Clarified, Add to It: Agree or Disagree and Say Why

Once students are sure they understand the speaker's comment, they should use think time to decide if they agree or disagree and why. Discussions should follow a flow; disjointed and unconnected comments don't constitute a "discussion." Rather, student comments should add to or build on the preceding comment. When students want to introduce a new topic, they should use a transition that helps all participants see a link between their comment and a previous one.

This move to agree or disagree does not apply to teachers—only to students. At this point in a student-driven discussion, there should be little if any feedback from the teacher, as students' comments will likely be influenced by the teacher's opinions. During the previously mentioned Roundtable discussion on trust, the students all looked to their teacher. "Tell us what you think," they pleaded. "*Please* tell us!" However, they knew Ms. Olcott would not respond. Her procedure is to never share her personal opinions with students—before, during, or after a discussion. She does not want to influence the content of *what* they think. Rather, her focus is on *how* they think—that is, their cognitive processing. Do they express themselves clearly? Do they listen to other points of view with an open mind? Do they refine their thinking throughout the course of the discussion? Do they use evidence to back up their opinions? Do they have open minds? These are discussion skills students can use for the rest of their lives, regardless of the content or focus.

Ask for Evidence

A true discussion in school does not mean "anything goes." It's not an opportunity to share unsubstantiated opinions or beliefs, without questioning them. Especially important, students should learn to consider which of their deeply held personal beliefs might cause them to see and hear only what reinforces those beliefs. (Refer to the Ladder of Inferences presented in Chapter 2.) When a discussion is text-based, it's easy to ask, "What evidence do you have for that statement from the text?" But it's equally important to ask for evidence when the discussion is more general, bringing together what has been studied over time in a unit or addressing issues that may be controversial in nature.

In a 7th grade class discussion, following the reading of *My Brother Sam Is Dead*, the teacher asked, "What would you have done? Would you have disobeyed your father and gone off to war?" A student made the following claim: "I wouldn't have been 18 years old before the end of the war. I couldn't have fought." None of the students questioned his belief that one had to be 18 to fight at the time of the Revolutionary War. The discussion quickly moved from this to other topics, so the teacher didn't have an opportunity to interject or question his evidence. When this happens during discussion, it provides the teacher with a substantive example to reinforce the importance of questioning facts that seem unsound. It might become a focus skill for the next student-led discussion: *Poses questions to clarify the thinking or reasoning behind an argument or conclusion.*

Ask Questions About Things That Puzzle You

The best way to engage actively in discussion is to think from a mindset of "not knowing." This allows one to be open to listening to others' points of view and seeking to better understand them. More important, a speaker who voices a true question extends an invitation for others to think about it and share their thoughts with the group.

In the middle of a discussion focused on a student-generated question about whether globalization is good or bad, Leigh Stovall and Erin McGuyar's 7th grade students at Hewitt-Trussville Middle School (AL) identified some of the popularized pros and cons. Many of the arguments made by these middle schoolers *against* globalization focused on the poor working conditions in developing countries, where workers are paid low wages to produce goods that would be bought primarily by wealthier American consumers. In the middle of this discussion, a lightbulb seemed to go off in one student's head as he interjected, "I have a question." He paused to think before continuing, "How come these people in other countries make such low money and don't make the same money as we do in this country? They're doing the same things we do." As he spoke, there was a real wondering in his voice, confirming that the previous comments had provoked this question. Students turned their thoughts to this question. Rather than glibly making comments about how people were suffering from low wages, it seemed to change the thinking to focus on *Why, indeed, is there such a discrepancy between the pay in our country and in developing countries?*

Correct Mistakes of Fact or Misconceptions

As with other tasks in the "sustaining" portion of a discussion, teachers hope that students will correct mistakes of fact. If they don't step forward to do this, however, the teacher must intervene by asking a question such as "What is your evidence for this statement?" or "Let's look together at the text, in the third paragraph of page 160. What is the author saying?"

Here's an example of how a skillful teacher corrected a misstatement during a discussion. In the middle of a culminating discussion about change, in which the students had actively read, formulated questions, and talked together over the course of four days about Martin Luther King, Jim Crow laws in the South, and Mahatma Gandhi's use of civil disobedience in overthrowing the British, teacher Eunice Davis (Ft. Worth ISD, TX) opened the floor for discussion by telling her 2nd graders, "Now we will open it up for discussion . . . if you have comments you want to make about Martin Luther King—or if you have questions, you can pose them now."

Student: "It's sort of about Martin Luther King but it's also about Mahatma Gandhi and the British." [Getting Ms. Davis's OK to proceed, the student continued.] "I think you can connect that Mahatma Gandhi was sort of like God because he spread peace and he made the Indians happy and the British were sort of like the devil because they were being mean and they were taking away rights, and so Mahatma Gandhi did civil disobedience and boycotted . . . in order to bring about change." [pause]

Teacher: "Would you say that the British were like devils—or did they just do evil things?"

Student: "They did evil things."

Teacher: "The things they did were evil. But we don't want to call them devils. The things they did were . . ." [pauses for student to complete sentence]

Student: "Evil." [The student smiles as she says this, as if in acknowledgement that her teacher was giving her a more correct way to say her thought.]

Teacher: "And the things that Gandhi did were like what God would do: kind things. Things that are kind for humanity. Is that what you were saying?"

[The student proudly nods and smiles to confirm the teacher's correct interpretation of her meaning.]

Now consider another example from the 7th grade social studies class (in Trussville, AL) where the students are a bit more sophisticated and the mistake more obvious to those paying attention. The outer circle had taken the inside position to discuss. The teacher had asked the first inside circle, "What are some of the *benefits* of globalization?" She began the second group with a different question, "What are some of the *costs* of globalization? Not just economic costs, but consider other costs as well." After a pause, one student replied, "It helps all the different countries stay in touch with one another and benefit from each other."

In the face of this response, which didn't address the question, many teachers would automatically repeat the question, ask the student to explain what the question meant, or interject, "If I had asked you the benefits of globalization, which the last group was discussing, your comment would have been right on target. But I asked, 'What are some of the costs?' Can you give a response to this question?" However, this teacher made none of those moves. She wisely remained quiet to see if the responder would self-correct or if another student would intervene.

The next student to speak added tactfully, "I agree with what you're saying. But also, the countries could get mad at one another—or jealous or something—so it could help them or it could be bad." A third student entered and explained that, yes, there are benefits that countries derive from globalization, "but there are also costs, such as people working for very low wages in factories that have bad conditions." Yet a fourth student weighed in: "I agree because of the working conditions." All eight students in the group commented. Finally, without prompting, the first student summed up this part of the discussion, "OK. So there are definitely pros and cons of globalization."

Nobody actually told this student outright that he had misunderstood the question, yet he provided a summary statement that acknowledged he understood there are costs involved. The teacher never intervened to correct the student. Think of how different this experience is compared to the Initiate-Response-Evaluate model of traditional classroom questioning, where students get immediate feedback, always from the teacher.

Aim for Equity in Participation

In a large group discussion of 25–30 students, it is highly unlikely that everyone will have an equal opportunity to participate. Time probably will not allow. If some students are monopolizing the conversation, the report from the "comment counter" will expose this, and students might set a goal for the next discussion, from norms such as "Share what you are thinking so others can learn from you" or "Monitor your talk so as not to monopolize the conversation." Some teachers use the strategy of giving every student three tokens—every comment costing one—and when they are used up, that student can't speak any more during the discussion. Copeland (2005) reports that such strategies seem to stifle the regular flow of conversation and that students don't like it. He recommends using it only rarely.

In Ms. Boyd's 7th grade ELA classroom at Joseph Cavallaro IS 281 in Brooklyn, New York, where students had accepted the responsibility to ensure that all voices were heard, students prompted other students to engage by making the following comments during a 15-minute discussion:

- To a student who had not spoken: "Omar, I'd like to hear what you're thinking."
- "I'd like to clarify what Adrianne said. Can you say more about that?"

- To another student who hadn't yet spoken: "I'd like to hear what Joseph is thinking about this idea."
- "I'd like for you to extend on that comment and let us know if you agree or disagree."

The use of an inside-outside circle engages a relatively higher percentage of students in the discussion by virtue of the fact that the groups are smaller. Yet another technique, as modeled by English teacher Christina Procter in a Teaching Channel video, "Socratic Seminar: Supporting Claims and Counterclaims" (2012) engages students, as a warm-up, to discuss in small groups. One student from each group then moves to a fishbowl in the center of the room to continue the discussion. The group uses a stuffed animal as its talking stick; no one can speak unless he or she is holding it. (Students seem to enjoy having something to do with their hands as they talk.) The teacher requires a second person from every team to replace the first so that the class hears at least two comments from each group. The teacher allots extra credit to groups that send in all members to speak. This certainly helps scaffold the notion of "hearing from everyone." Many of the small-group structures described in Chapter 4 also scaffold this behavior.

Closing

Whether discussion is teacher-facilitated, conducted in small groups, or student-driven, students should consolidate their learning as the discussion closes. Teachers typically regain the "driver's seat" to facilitate closing reflections. In the Roundtable discussion referenced earlier in this chapter, about 10 minutes before the end of the 90-minute block, the teacher said, "I'd like for you to share a reflection: an idea, a quote, or a question. [pause] We'll ask Maria to begin, and we'll go around the circle, hearing from everyone." Here are a few of the student reflections:

- "I was thinking—everything we've talked about in Roundtable this year—they're all related: responsibility, trust, respect, hate, love. I'm just wondering: What is at the center?"

- "How can you really trust close family members?"
- "Being trusted is a greater compliment than being loved."
- "Is there a difference between believing in something and trusting in something?"
- "I think I know what is at the center that Michael asked about: I think it is yourself."

Students had engaged in deep thinking—listening to, analyzing, and evaluating their own and peers' thinking. They shared openly in a classroom that fostered trust and community; they formulated questions; and they spoke, as moved, about their own and others' thoughts. The previous discussion took place during the last period of the school day. Twenty minutes after class, six students remained in the classroom to continue the discussion!

Sometimes teachers ask for written thoughts and have students turn them in as exit passes. After a discussion about two poems titled "Democracy" (one by Langston Hughes and one by Sara Holbrook), Ms. Mohassib, a 7th grade English teacher at Joseph Cavallaro IS 281 in Brooklyn, New York, prompted students to summarize their discussion in writing. "Many of us were talking about what we learned from these two texts and applying it to our lives today. What insights or deeper understandings did you gain from these readings? Individually respond to the questions on your handout." (See Figure 5.6.) She asked that students begin reflecting at the end of the period and bring their completed reflections to turn in the next day.

Reflecting

In this stage of the discussion, the teacher usually maintains a leadership role while facilitating a reflective discussion or giving directions for written assessments and reflections. Students have the responsibility to honestly reflect, assess, and comment on the quality of the discussion and to supply evidence to back up their feedback. Following are formats for reflecting (1) after a large-group discussion, (2) after small-group discussions, and (3) after inside-outside circles.

Three Keys to Meaningful Feedback

1. Is specific, providing examples as appropriate.
2. Pertains to targeted discussion skill or criteria.
3. Helps establish goals for the next discussion.

Figure 5.6 | **Student Self-Reflection on Learning**

Name: _____ Date: _____ Period: _____

1. What did you talk about today that reinforced what you already knew?
I knew that we live in a democracy but I didn't know how big the government is.

2. What new ideas (or different ways of thinking) did you encounter?
I learned that some people see the unfairness about race; others think it is poverty, not race.

3. What questions, wonderings, or puzzles do you have about the content we discussed?
What can help make democracy work better?

4. Which identified discussion skills did you use intentionally and effectively?
I added on to two different comments.

5. What, if anything, would you like to do better during future discussions?
I would like to ask my question and hear what others think about it.

Note that if students are to assess and reflect on the quality of the discussion, they need to understand what constitutes meaningful feedback. First, it should be specific. General feedback such as "It was a good discussion" isn't meaningful because it doesn't specify what made the discussion good. Here are examples of specific feedback: "The students were helping to keep everybody accountable, like when Jose asked Cynthia where the evidence for her comment came from" or "It seemed like this group had all prepared because I counted five references to the text, and three of them were quotes." Second, meaningful feedback connects to specific criteria that students are aware of in advance. For example, if the focus discussion skill is "'Piggybacks' and elaborates on class-mates' comments," a student might say, "I heard three instances of students adding on, like when Samantha added on to Lilly's comment by saying that she thought Lilly's way was one way to solve the problem, but that she did it a different way. And then she explained her method." Finally, if feedback is to be meaningful, students should provide suggestions for how the discussion could be improved. The major purpose is to establish goals for the next discussion.

After a Large-Group Discussion

Here's another example from Ms. Mohassib's classroom, where students were using a four-second think time for the first time in discussion. The teacher ended the discussion by reflecting aloud about the silence: "During today's discussion, we used a four-second delay to give everyone time to think about what had been said. What did the use of silence add to our discussion?" One student said, "I think it's helpful because sometimes people just interrupt—or you don't take time to think about what they said." Another added, "I didn't like it because I forgot what I was going to say." One commented, "I was counting to four, but then somebody started talking before I got to four." Another said, "I agree with Michael that it didn't work out. I forgot to count, and others forgot, too." The teacher continued, "Keep in mind that when we try something new, we may need to practice before we become comfortable with it. What could we do to improve our use of this silent time to think?" The students offered three suggestions: "Maybe we should write it down so we don't forget what we want to say," "Show a hand signal when you're done thinking," and "Some people count faster than others."

For more in-depth and personal reflection after the class has engaged in discussion three or four times, a teacher might use a protocol such as Reflective Questioning: The teacher presents two reflective questions on the day following a discussion and gives students time to reflect individually and to write their responses. For example, the teacher might present these questions:

1. What did you do yesterday to enhance the quality of the group's discussion? Give specific examples and use the list of posted skills to help you frame your thinking and writing.
2. What were the benefits of the group discussion to your understanding of the text (or topic)? What might you or others have done to enhance this understanding?

After the students write their responses, they gather in groups of three to engage in the Reflective Questioning process. Each group member chooses one of three roles: Interviewer, Reflector, or Observer. The Interviewer begins by asking a question of the Reflector, using good questioning and listening strategies (e.g., "What were some ways you contributed to the group's discussion?"), maintaining eye contact and leaning forward, allowing the Reflector to speak without interruption, and asking, "What might have happened if . . . ?" or "Can you give an example?"). The Reflector speaks honestly to the Interviewer for three to five minutes, as the Interviewer attempts to elicit reflective comments. During this time, the Observer records what the Interviewer says and does to encourage reflection and deeper thinking. When time is called, the Observer gives feedback. Then the students switch roles and repeat the process two more times.

After a Small-Group Discussion

The teacher may prepare brief assessment forms (like one suggested in Chapter 3, Figure 3.5) and ask students to assess individual contributions and overall group functioning related to the learning targets and designated discussion skills.

After Inside-Outside Circles

There are many different ways of asking the outside (observer) circles to give feedback. If students are assigned to watch particular students in the inside circle, they can coach those students, one-on-one, during the interim period between the discussion of the first and second groups. Typically, the two students (coach and discussant) get together and talk about what each believes the inside circle member accomplished toward meeting his or her discussion goals. Together they talk about how the discussant might improve to meet his or her goals.

If the outside circle is asked to observe the entire group, taking notes on exemplary discussion moves and on the progress of the discussion, the teacher asks those students what they saw (examples or nonexamples) related to particular discussion goals. One way to do this is through use of a modified version of the Tuning Protocol from the National School Reform Faculty (http://www.nsrfharmony.org/system/files/protocols/tuning_0.pdf). This protocol holds every observer accountable to contribute and engages every student in thinking about and giving feedback.

First, the teacher poses the following question:

> Look at the notes you took while you observed this discussion. Identify one piece of positive feedback for the group—or for an individual—that is based on either (1) the quality of the discussion (discussion skills) or (2) the content of the discussion—that is, something that enhanced your understanding of the subject under discussion. Be prepared to be specific.

After a minute of reflection, the teacher calls on a student to begin with one sentence of positive feedback. Moving quickly around the circle, each student contributes one piece of feedback. The teacher prompts, "Now think about the discussion and ways we might improve it next time. Again, I'd like everyone in the outer circle to contribute and to say it in a sentence." The teacher selects a different student to begin this time, moving around the circle quickly before asking for comments from the inner circle.

Too often, when people give feedback, they tend to think of "ways to improve" rather than "what you did well." However, because this protocol begins with positive or "warm" feedback, students are more receptive to the "cool" feedback that follows, which addresses areas of improvement. The use of such a protocol also ensures equity of participation: each student speaks and is limited to one sentence.

Questioning Practices

All four of the questioning practices detailed in Chapter 1 are essential for student-driven discussion: (1) A compelling question that interests students and suggests diverse points of view helps the discussion take off. (2) Equity in responding is important because it is through talking that students clarify their thinking. If some are not speaking, they may be thinking, but probably not as deeply as their classmates who are thinking aloud. (3) Moves to scaffold peers' thinking—through listening, asking probing questions, and using silence to think—make the discussion a "discussion" rather than a recitation of one fact or question after another. (4) A culture of thoughtfulness, respect for one another, and valuing of the discussion process helps to create trust and support students' participation.

"Students must feel intellectually safe with the teacher and each other. Respect must be modeled, taught, and practiced—over and over. Only then can teachers and students reap the intellectual, academic, and affective rewards of rich classroom discussions" (Erdmann & Metzger, 2013, p. 104).

In student-driven discussion, the most essential questioning practice is the creation of a classroom environment that supports thoughtful and respectful discourse: a safe environment in which students are comfortable articulating their own beliefs and are able to disagree respectfully, pose true questions, and risk "going out on a limb." When this kind of discussion occurs weekly or twice-monthly, students develop a deep commitment to the classmates with whom they discuss. They look forward to the opportunity to learn from one another. Their commitment to the group motivates them to prepare for a rigorous discussion, to listen carefully, and to weigh their thoughts against their classmates'. They develop a meaningful camaraderie; they trust their classmates as much as trust develops in a "team" that works together over time to set and meet difficult goals. This safe environment develops only through the experience of discussing within a trusting, caring, and academically rigorous community of thinkers and learners.

Reflecting and Connecting

1. Figure 5.1 identifies and describes different approaches to student-driven discussion. *Which do you believe to be the "best fit" for your students? Why?*
2. Review the teacher responsibilities that appear throughout this chapter (listed in Figures 5.3, 5.4, and 5.5). *Which ones seem most challenging to you? Why?*
3. Review the student responsibilities that appear throughout this chapter (in Figures 5.3, 5.4, and 5.5). *Which ones do you believe will be most challenging for your students? Why?*
4. *Given your past use of student-driven discussion, what steps can you take to work with your students to move this form of discussion to the next level?*

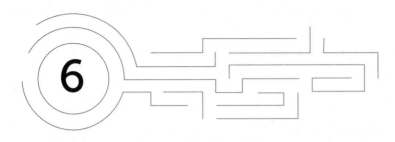

Questioning for Discussion: Creating Your Own Designs

How will you orchestrate questioning for discussion in support of learning for your students?

Quality questioning and disciplined discussion look and sound different from classroom to classroom. But where these two practices thrive, teachers and students are working together to develop patterns of interaction that support student learning in the knowledge, cognitive, and—perhaps most important— social domains. The patterns that emerge reflect the character of the teacher and the individual students who make up a classroom community. And because both questioning and discussion are processes, they are ever changing and, we hope, ever improving.

This book offers resources teachers can use to create designs that build on their own and their students' strengths and embody appropriate expectations for students. As we come to a close, we invite you to reflect on the frameworks we've presented and consider *if, for what purposes, how*, and *when* you will apply *which* of these in your setting. These are tools we hope you can use as you make decisions about how best to engage your students in deep and meaningful learning.

Three Forms of Discussion: Deciding When to Use Which

Discussion occurs in multiple settings or arenas, depending upon instructional purpose, teacher expertise, and students' developmental levels. Three forms of discussion—teacher-guided, structured small-group, and student-driven—are explained, respectively, in Chapters 3, 4, and 5. As you plan for discussion, you might view these as three options to choose from. The option you select will vary with the depth of student knowledge about the proposed discussion topic, students' skill level, and the instructional purpose.

Teachers are initially the orchestrators of questioning and discussion for their students. Beginning with teacher-guided discussions, we create a "musical score" of sorts that matches the developmental level of our students and the demands of the content area or discipline in play. We model dispositions and behaviors and offer opportunities for students to practice the social, cognitive, and use-of-knowledge skills that produce a disciplined and meaningful discussion. We strive to bring all voices into play—knowing this will result in both harmony and discord. In this context, teachers play a primary role, not only through modeling, but also by scaffolding with statements, strategic questions, and other supportive strategies. In this setting, we can stop to coach individuals and the whole group.

While one could infer that teacher-guided discussion is primarily for use with students who are just learning to discuss, this is not the case. Teacher-guided is also a preferred form when students are in the earlier stages of mastering content, when they need teacher scaffolding of knowledge and can also benefit from an explicit focus on selected discussion skills. In fact, we view teacher-guided discussion as the workhorse of classroom learning, a form that has a place at all grade levels, in all content areas, with all ages and developmental levels of students—and in every stage of learning.

Structured small groups can be used to reinforce and extend student learning of the skills and processes spotlighted in teacher-guided discussions, while affording students opportunities to deepen their knowledge related to a content-area learning target. This arena can be viewed as a practice field where students follow a particular playbook created by their teacher to refine skills required for a more free-flowing discussion. Again, teachers orchestrate the sessions by choosing the structure or protocol that fits the instructional purpose and scaffolding the discussion skills on which students are working. The protocols scaffold thinking and participation, freeing the teacher to monitor and intervene with coaching, as necessary, or to guide the discussion of one of the small groups, if this type of differentiation is appropriate. Again, this form of discussion never outwears its usefulness for student learning. In Chapter 4, we highlighted the different instructional purposes for which structured small-group discussions can be employed, along with the specific discussion skills they scaffold. Both of these variables inform the protocol of choice for a particular lesson.

If teacher-guided discussion calls to mind an orchestra, student-driven discussions can be thought of as jazz. When students inquire into a given topic or issue independent of teacher guidance and intervention, they literally "play off one another" as they engage in dialogue that creates a broader pool of knowledge and deepens individual understandings. The argument in this book is that students don't naturally possess the skills required to make this form of discussion productive. As in a jazz band, students need to learn to listen deeply to one another and respond in ways that contribute to the creation of a whole that is much greater than the sum of its parts.

Participation in both teacher-guided and structured small-group discussions can help prepare students for student-driven forms. You may be wondering when your students will be ready for such independent talk, and how long they will need to practice through engagement in the other two forms. The timing for such a discussion is certainly a matter of teacher judgment. We believe, however, that almost all students can productively participate in student-driven discussions if they have exemplars that help them understand their roles and responsibilities and if they partner with their teachers in planning the focus and parameters of their discussion so as to develop true ownership.

Within every unit of study, a teacher can productively incorporate all three forms of discussion. As you begin planning a new unit, you might take the long view, considering at which points one or more of these forms would add value to learning and provide opportunity for student development of related discussion skills. We can imagine strategic use of teacher-guided and structured small-group discussions all along the learning pathway. Student-driven discussion may occur less frequently, but hopefully often enough to allow students to develop the independence this form supports. It is through the blending of all three forms of discussion that we can design experiences for our students that will enable them to develop discussion skills while truly mastering content.

Three Sets of Skills: Identifying the Right Mix for Your Students

Chapter 2 offers a full complement of discussion skills, which we organize into three categories: social, cognitive, and use of knowledge. In all, we have identified more than 40 skills that support positive and productive student interaction. We would never imagine presenting all of these skills to a class of students. Certainly this would be overwhelming to both the teacher and students. We resisted the temptation to develop a scope and sequence of skills because we believe the value of such a tool comes from a faculty who collaborate to create this kind of product for schoolwide use. Our vision is that teachers will use our compendium of skills as input to a continuum of skills across the grade levels in their school.

Absent such a continuum in your school, how do individual teachers proceed in selecting the skills that will most benefit students in a given class? We offer the following approach for your consideration. If possible, work through this process with others who share your teaching assignment.

- Review the skills we offered in Chapter 2 (and summarized in Appendix A), and reflect on what you might expect from your students, given what you know about students of this age/grade level from prior experience. Which have been strengths of past students that you might need only to reinforce for the majority of your students? Which ones do you believe are within the zone of proximal development (ZPD) of most students? Which do you believe to be beyond the grasp of most students at this developmental level?

- Select the skills that are most critical for the discipline or content areas you teach. If you teach multiple subjects, make the selection for each separately.
- Develop a draft list of skills emerging from the first two exercises, and involve your students in a pre-assessment. You might develop a simple survey and have students rate themselves on each skill. Additionally, you can record your class during a discussion and look for evidence of use of the identified skills. Share with colleagues.
- Depending upon the number and nature of selected skills, arrange them in a sequence from "most accessible" to your students to "most challenging." Use this as a resource when planning any one of the identified forms of discussion.

Intentionality and strategic planning are essential if we are to help students become more proficient in skills required for disciplined discussion. This can yield great benefits to your students.

Early on, we argued that development of skills for discussion is both a means and an end of learning. Certainly, students extend and deepen their understandings of a discipline through engagement in collaborative learning (social skills) propelled by disciplined thinking (cognitive skills) and grounded in a solid knowledge base (use-of-knowledge skills). Hence, skills for discussion contribute to the mastery of content goals. Likewise, as students improve their social skills, sharpen their cognitive skills, and enhance their ability to use knowledge, they are developing their capacity as life-long learners and, equally important, productive members of our democratic society. They will not take us with them as they leave our classrooms. They will be operating independently. So, we believe it is important to design opportunities for students of all skill and ability levels to enhance their competency across all three skills sets. And, we are convinced that students are more likely to internalize these behaviors if they develop parallel dispositions that reinforce and support these skills.

Five Stages of the Discussion Process: Planning for Success

One of the themes of this book is that good discussions don't just happen. Teachers plan for and orchestrate them, and students prepare for and make them their own. In Chapter 3, in the context of teacher-guided discussion, we introduced a cycle for thinking about and planning for productive discussions. We referred to the five stages embedded in this cycle as we engaged you in thinking about structured small-group discussions (Chapter 4) and student-driven discussions (Chapter 5). "Preparing" and "Reflecting" are the bookends of this cycle, and they can serve as a feedback loop that facilitates learning from and improving discussions as they occur over time. By feeding forward information gleaned from reflections to the preparation of subsequent discussions, we can continue to stretch our students by challenging them to ever-higher levels of proficiency. With the inclusion of the Opening, Sustaining, and Closing stages in the cycle, we acknowledge the importance of anticipating and planning for what might occur during the body of the discussion itself. While we can never forecast the exact turns a discussion may take, we can predict and plan for possible student moves and probable challenges.

When using the five-state discussion cycle as a template to design structured small-group and student-driven discussions, we can be more intentional in our thinking about ways to shift some of the responsibility and ownership for a discussion to students. To the extent that we strategically involve students in preparing for a discussion, we can expect them to be more authentically engaged and accountable for outcomes. We encourage you to share this cycle with older students and to talk with them about ways they can contribute to a successful discussion. A spin-off benefit of making the discussion process transparent to students is the opportunity for them to become more mindful and metacognitive when they approach discussions within and outside school.

Four Quality Questioning Practices:
Using the Tools of Inquiry

Quality questioning and productive discussion are so closely intertwined that it becomes difficult to separate the two. In Chapter 1, we highlighted four components of quality questioning that are essential for a productive discussion: framing a focus question, promoting equitable participation, scaffolding student thinking and speaking, and creating a culture that supports thoughtful and respectful discourse. These four featured prominently in subsequent chapters.

In our early work with teachers, we focused attention on developing teaching practices in these four areas (Walsh & Sattes, 2005); in more recent years, we have emphasized the importance of teachers partnering with students to develop their own and student skills in the questioning process (Walsh & Sattes, 2011). A productive discussion results only when the teacher and the students are in true partnership and when students themselves master these components of quality questioning.

Consider ways you can engage students as you frame a focus question for discussion. Begin with the identification of a core issue or topic that is relevant and potentially important to students. Ask students what interests or puzzles them about key concepts, and use their input in determining the focus for the discussion question. Or invite students to help frame discussion questions. Students can be valuable members of curriculum design teams. Ideally, they will be the chief architects of questions for student-driven discussion.

The quality of a discussion question affects the level of student interest and ownership in the emerging discourse. However, even a very compelling question will not, in and of itself, break long-established patterns of classroom participation. Students must truly believe that a question is open for discussion, not a prompt to discover what the teacher believes about a topic or issue. As teachers, we must be both intentional and persistent in communicating to students our expectation that they all have something worthy to contribute to the broader understanding of an important issue. Moreover, teachers must be steadfast in expecting and facilitating participation by all students. A number of the collaborative skills and supportive dispositions seek to develop student proficiency in promoting equitable participation. When students understand the reasons for and value of equitable participation, it can develop into a classroom norm that helps create a culture in which discussions can thrive.

Scaffolding, the third component of quality questioning, is a frequently used word in this book. In teacher-guided instruction, we examined specific actions teachers can use when building student knowledge and skills. Many of these behaviors appear as student skills for discussion in Chapter 2. Student-driven discussions work when students scaffold one another's thinking by paraphrasing and revoicing, posing questions, and building on another's ideas. In this context they use this quality questioning practice to deepen their own and others' understanding, raise important questions, and explore new territory.

Teachers cannot, by themselves, create cultures that support thoughtful and respectful discourse. Culture is born from the collective norms and behaviors of all community members. However, as teachers, we can hold forth a vision for the kind of culture we hope to co-create with students. We can also identify norms and behaviors associated with such cultures and model these with great intentionality. We can offer students exemplars—and nonexamples. We can provide feedback as we observe and coach individual students. But at the end of the day, it is our students who must demonstrate respect for one another's perspectives, honor time for thinking by all, exhibit curiosity, persevere in searching for deeper meaning, encourage and reinforce one another, and in myriad other ways create a culture that is hospitable to authentic, respectful, and thoughtful discourse—and to quality questioning.

One Final Question: Reflecting on Your Beliefs

You are the one who will ultimately decide whether or not discussion holds potential for your students. It's worth repeating: Productive discussions don't just happen. They occur because teachers believe discussions enable students to think more deeply about content and to achieve desired social and cognitive outcomes. They happen because teachers believe it is worth their time and effort to plan for and dedicate class time to discussions, to design a unit of study that strategically incorporates one or more forms of discussion into the learning cycle. If you believe there is value in discussion, we hope this book will assist you and your students in weaving discussions that both advance academic goals and prepare students for life in our democratic society. We can imagine no more beautiful a tapestry.

APPENDIX A

Skills Associated with Disciplined Discussion

Social Skills
Speaking Skills • Speaks clearly and loudly enough that everyone can hear. • Speaks when there is an opening in the discussion, without raising a hand. • Speaks to classmates as well as to the teacher. • Speaks in complete sentences. • Contributes to the discussion so that all can learn from him or her. • Expresses own ideas clearly. • Speaks at length so that thinking is visible to others. • Paraphrases portions of a text or information presented in other formats.
Listening Skills • Uses silence after a classmate stops speaking to think about what the speaker said and to compare the speaker's thinking to one's own. • Asks questions to better understand the speaker's point of view. • Waits before adding one's own ideas to ensure that the speaker has completed his or her thoughts. • Accurately paraphrases what another student says. • Looks at the speaking student and gives nonverbal cues that one is paying attention.
Collaborating Skills • "Piggybacks" and elaborates on classmates' comments. • Actively seeks to include classmates who are not participating. • Responds to classmates' questions nondefensively. • Remains open to ideas that are different from one's own. • Actively seeks to understand and communicate with individuals who have different backgrounds and perspectives. • Disagrees in a civil and respectful manner.

Cognitive Skills
Connection-Making Skills • Identifies similarities and differences between one's own ideas and those of others. • Relates prior knowledge (both academic and personal) to the topic of discussion. • Offers reasons and textual evidence to support one's own point of view. • Analyzes and evaluates information from difference sources.
Questioning Skills • Poses questions to clarify and better understand the substance of a topic or text. • Asks questions to identify a speaker's assumptions. • Poses questions to clarify the thinking or reasoning behind an argument or conclusion. • Surfaces and questions own assumptions. • Asks questions when curious. • Asks "what if" questions to encourage divergent thinking.
Creating Skills • Draws inferences from different speakers' ideas that take the conversation to a deeper level. • Integrates information from multiple sources to produce a new way of thinking. • Suspends judgment while listening to a new solution or interpretation from a classmate. • Contributes to the building of collaborative solution.

Use-of-Knowledge Skills
General/Relate to All Spheres of Knowledge • Strives for accuracy in presentation of facts. • Cites information sources. • Evaluates the credibility of information sources. • Relates comments to the subject or question for discussion; does not get off topic.
Text-Based Knowledge • Evidences serious preparation for discussion by referring to texts and related research or to other media (e.g., a work from visual art or music). • Cites specific evidence from the text or other sources. • Integrates evidence from multiple texts or sources into one's argument. • Uses academic vocabulary and the language of the discipline.
Prior Academic Knowledge • Draws relevant information from prior learning in the subject area (discipline) under study. • Draws relevant information from other subject areas.
Experiential Knowledge • Introduces relevant information from out-of-school sources. • Reflects on and evaluates personal beliefs or positions on issues in relation to ideas offered in a discussion. • Connects current social, economic, or cultural phenomena to academic content on which the discussion is focused. • Assesses appropriateness of information to the classroom arena.

APPENDIX B

Template for Planning a Productive Discussion

I. Framing the Focus Question for Discussion

A. Issue or Key Concept

1. To which standards does this relate?
2. To what extent does the issue invite multiple perspectives or points of view?
3. To what extent do the students possess the breadth and depth of knowledge required to think about the issue?
4. In what ways might this issue engage students? To what extent does the issue relate to student interests? Why might it seem important or relevant to these students?

B. Wording and Structure of the Question

1. What academic vocabulary is embedded in the question?
2. What verb (or verbs) will activate the desired depth of thinking?
3. Would a context-setting preamble, such as a lead-in sentence, help focus and activate student thinking? If so, what might that be?

II. Selecting Discussion Skills and Dispositions

A. Social Skills. Consider your students' current proficiencies in speaking, listening, and collaborative thinking. If most students in your class have not mastered these fundamental social skills, the primary focus for this discussion should be on social skills alone. If most of your students demonstrate mastery of core social skills, select up to three of these for review and reinforcement—and target skills from another of the categories.

1.
2.
3.

B. **Cognitive Skills.** Examine the focus question to help you decide which cognitive skills to target. Consider (1) the verbs in the focus question and (2) probable student responses. Select a limited number of cognitive skills, and be prepared to model them through think-alouds.

1.
2.
3.

C. **Use-of-Knowledge Skills.** Examine the focus question to help you decide which use-of-knowledge skills to target. For example, to what extent does the focus question invite students to integrate information from other disciplines or out-of-school experiences— or to access and evaluate multiple sources?

1.
2.

D. **Dispositions:** Select dispositions that reinforce the identified skills. Prepare to help students understand the connection between selected dispositions and related skills.

1.
2.

Prediscussion Preparation for Students

A. Reading from text or primary sources. Text-based discussions support student focus on the question for discussion by providing a point of reference for their thinking and accountability for their points of view.

B. Independent research on topics related to discussion. Given student access to online information sources, independent research is a viable form of pre-reading and can yield a diversity of viewpoints. When this is the selected mode for student preparation, certain use-of-knowledge skills, such as "evaluates the credibility of information sources," become very critical.

C. Prediscussion writing assignment. Writing assignments assist students in clarifying their thinking as they prepare for a discussion.

D. Student generation of questions related to a discussion topic. Students are more apt to pose questions during a discussion if they've had time to think about the topic in advance. A simple but powerful strategy is to preview the focus question the day before the discussion and invite students to generate true "wonderings" about the subject as a homework assignment.

III. Structures to Activate and Sustain Thinking and Speaking

A. Activation of Thinking

1. **Develop a prompt.** In a teacher-guided discussion, a prompt might invite students to engage in reflective writing before the discussion to establish focus and generate ideas. Effective prompts help students see the relevance of the topic to their lives.

2. **Select a structure**
   - **Online Platform.** Examples: Schoology, Edmodo, Moodle
   - **Paired Response.** Examples: Think-Pair-Share; Card Swap
   - **Small Group:** Examples: Synectic; People-Graph

B. Regaining Momentum, Focus, or Increasing Participation

1. **Anticipate problems** that might emerge in the discussion that would require a teacher intervention. Consider the four situations below, along with any others you anticipate, given your students and the topic.

   - What if the class seems to be losing energy or enthusiasm, or if the discussion doesn't appear to be moving forward or going deeper?
   - What if students do not stay focused on the discussion question, but continue to get off topic?
   - What if students are not using text-based evidence—or use erroneous information—to support their positions?
   - What if the majority of students are not speaking or participating?

2. **Possible Interventions**

   - Use of paired response, such as Think-Pair-Share or Turn and Talk (prepare prompts to use for this purpose).
   - Refocus by posing a variation on the opening question, one prepared in connection with original thinking about the focus question.
   - Provide time-out for individual consolidation of thinking and writing, perhaps with stipulation that each student think of a question he or she has about the conversation to this point.

IV. Organizational Issues

A. Size and Configuration of Discussion Group

1. **Whole Class**
2. **Fishbowl** (*Considerations: Number of students constituting each small discussion group, number of groups/rotations, and composition of groups*)

3. **Small groups facilitated by teacher** (*Considerations: Composition of each group, length of time for each small-group discussion, and directions to be given to students when they are engaged in a pre- or post-discussion activity*)

B. Floor Plan
   1. Large circle
   2. Inside-outside circles
   3. U-shaped
   4. Other:

REFERENCES

Adler, M. J. (1985). *How to speak, how to listen.* New York: Macmillan.

Argyris, C. (1990). *Overcoming organizational defenses: Facilitating organizational learning.* Boston: Allyn & Bacon.

Applebee, A. N. (2003). *The language of literature.* New York: McDougal.

Block, P. (2011). *Flawless consulting: A guide to getting your expertise used* (3rd ed.). San Francisco: Jossey-Bass.

Boyd, M., & Galda, L. (2011). *Real talk in elementary classrooms: Effective oral language practice.* New York: Guilford.

Boyer, E. L. (1983). *High school: A report on secondary education in America.* New York: Joanna Cotler Books.

Bridges, D. (1979). *Education, democracy and discussion.* Windsor, UK: NFER Publishing.

Brookfield, S. D., & Preskill, S. (2005). *Discussion as a way of teaching: Tools and techniques for democratic classrooms* (2nd ed.). San Francisco: Jossey-Bass.

Brown, J., & Isaacs, D. (2005). *The world café: Shaping our futures through conversations that matter.* Oakland, CA: Berrett-Koehler.

Cartier, J. L., Smith, M. S., Stein, M. K., & Ross, D. K. (2013). *5 practices for orchestrating productive task-based discussions in science.* Reston, VA: National Council of Teachers of Mathematics.

Cazden, C. B. (2001). *Classroom discourse: The language of teaching and learning* (2nd ed.). Portsmouth, NH: Heinemann.

Conley, D. T. (2008). *College knowledge: What it really takes for students to succeed and what we can do to get them ready.* San Francisco: Jossey-Bass.

Copeland, M. (2005). *Socratic circles: Fostering critical and creative thinking in middle and high school.* Portland, MN: Stenhouse.

Costa, A. L., & Kallick, B. (2014). *Dispositions: Reframing teaching and learning.* Thousand Oaks, CA: Corwin.

Csikszentmihalyi, M. (1990). *Flow: The psychology of optimal experience.* New York: Harper & Row.

Danielson, C. (2013). *The framework for teaching evaluation instrument, 2013 edition.* Princeton, NJ: The Danielson Group.

Dillon, J. T. (1988). *Questioning and teaching: A manual of practice.* New York: Teachers College Press.

Dillon, J. T. (1994). *Using discussion in the classroom.* Buckingham, UK: Open University Press.

Donoahue, Z. (2001). Examination of the development of classroom community through class meetings. In G. Well (Ed.), *Action talk and text: Learning and teaching through inquiry* (pp. 25–40). New York: Teachers College Press.

Duckworth, E. (1981). *Understanding children's understandings.* Paper presented at the Ontario Institute for Studies in Education, Toronto, Canada.

Erdmann, A., & Metzger, M. (2013). Discussion in practice: Sharing our learning curve. In J. Ippolito, J. F. Lawrence, & C. Zallar (Eds.), *Adolescent literacy in the era of the Common Core: From research into practice* (pp. 103–116). Cambridge, MA: Harvard Education Press.

Fisher, D., & Frey, N. (2008). *Content-area conversations: How to plan discussion-based lessons for diverse language learners.* Alexandria, VA: ASCD.

Fry, E. B., & Kress, J. E. (2006). *The reading teacher's book of lists: Grades K–12* (5th ed.). San Francisco: Jossey-Bass.

Goodlad, J. (1984). *A place called school.* New York: McGraw-Hill.

Graff, G. (2004). *Clueless in academe: How schooling obscures the life of the mind.* Hartford, CT: Yale University Press.

Green, J. (2002). *The green book of songs by subject: The thematic guide to popular music.* Nashville, TN: Professional Desk References.

Hale, A. S., & City, A. C. (2006). *The teacher's guide to leading student-centered discussions: Talking about texts in the classroom.* Thousand Oaks, CA: Corwin.

Hammond, W. D., & Nessel, D. D. (2011). *The comprehension experience: Engaging readers through effective inquiry and discussion.* Portsmouth, NH: Heinemann.

Haroutunian-Gordon, S. (2014). *Interpretive discussion: Engaging students in text-based conversations.* Cambridge, MA: Harvard Education Press.

Hess, D. (2011). Discussions that drive democracy. *Promoting Respectful Schools, 69*(1), 69–73.

Ho, A. D., & Kane, T. J. (2013). *The reliability of classroom observations by school personnel.* The MET Project. Seattle: Bill & Melinda Gates Foundation.

Isaacson, W. (2014). *The innovators: How a group of hackers, geniuses and geeks created the digital revolution.* New York: Simon & Schuster.

Juzwik, M. M., Borsheim-Black, C., Caughlan, S., & Heintz, A. (2013). *Inspiring dialogue: Talking to learn in the English classroom.* New York: Teachers College Press.

Kamil, M. L., Borman, G. D., Dole, J., Kral, C. C., Salinger, T., & Torgesen, J. (2008). *Improving adolescent literacy: Effective classroom and intervention practices.* Washington, DC: Institute for Education Sciences.

McCann, T. M. (2014). *Transforming talk into text: Argument writing, inquiry, and discussion, grades 6–12.* New York: Teachers College Press.

Mehan, H. (1979). *Learning lessons: Social organization in the classroom.* Cambridge, MA: Harvard University Press.

Michener, C. J., & Ford-Connors, E. (2013). Research in discussion: Effective support for literacy, content, and academic achievement. In J. Ippolito, J. Lawrence, & C. Zaller (Eds.), *Adolescent literacy in the era of the common core: From research into practice* (pp. 85–102). Cambridge, MA: Harvard Education Press.

Murphy, P. K., Wilkinson, I. A. G., Soter, A. O., Hennessey, M. N., & Alexander, J. F. (2009). Examining the effects of classroom discussion on students' comprehension of text: A meta-analysis. *Journal of Educational Psychology, 101*(3), 740–764.

Nystrand, M. (1997). Dialogic instruction: When recitation becomes conversation. In M. Nystrand, with A. Gamoran, R. Kachur, & C. Prendergast, Eds., *Opening dialogue: Understanding the dynamics of language and learning in the English classroom* (pp. 1–29). New York: Teachers College Press.

Nystrand, M., with Gamoran, A., Kachur, R., & Prendergast, C., Eds. (1997). *Opening dialogue: Understanding the dynamics of language and learning in the English classroom.* New York: Teachers College Press.

Perkins, D. N. (2010). *Making learning whole: How seven principles of teaching can transform education.* San Francisco: Jossey-Bass.

Popham, W. J. (2013). *Evaluating America's teachers: Mission possible?* Thousand Oaks, CA: Corwin.

Ritchhart, R., Church, M., & Morrison, K. (2011). *Making thinking visible: How to promote engagement, understanding, and independence for all learners.* San Francisco: Jossey-Bass.

Rowe, M. B. (1986, January–February). Wait time: Slowing down may be a way of speeding up! *Journal of Teacher Education, 37*(1), 43–50.

Sartain, L., Stoelinga, S.R., & Brown, E.R. (2011). *Rethinking teacher evaluation in Chicago: Lessons learned from classroom observations, principal-teacher conferences, and district implementation.* Chicago: Consortium on Chicago School Research at the University of Chicago Urban Education Institute.

Sawyer, R. K. (2009). The new science of learning. In R. K. Sawyer (Ed.), *The Cambridge handbook of the learning sciences* (pp. 1–16). Cambridge, UK: Cambridge University Press.

Schmoker, M. (2011). *Focus: Elevating the essentials to radically improve student learning.* Alexandria, VA: ASCD.

Smith, M. S., & Stein, M. K. (2011). *5 practices for orchestrating productive mathematics discussions.* Reston, VA: National Council of Teachers of Mathematics.

Teachers of English to Speakers of Other Languages (TESOL). (2006). *PreK–12 English language proficiency standards: Augmentation of the World-Class Design and Assessment (WIDA) consortium of English language proficiency standards.* Alexandria, VA: Author.

Teaching Channel. (2012). *Socratic seminar: Supporting claims and counterclaims* [Online video]. Retrieved from https://www.teachingchannel.org/videos/using-socratic-seminars-in-classroom.

Teaching Channel. (2013a). *Socratic seminar: The "n-word"* [Online video]. Retrieved from https://www.teachingchannel.org/videos/teaching-the-n-word.

Teaching Channel. (2013b). *Socratic seminars: Patience and practice* [Online video]. Retrieved from https://www.teachingchannel.org/videos/bring-socratic-seminars-to-the-classroom.

Teaching Channel. (2014). *Inquiry-based discussion* [Online video]. Retrieved from https://www.teachingchannel.org/videos/inquiry-based-discussions-for-text.

Teaching Channel. (2015). *Formative assessment: Collaborative discussions* [Online video]. Retrieved from https://www.teachingchannel.org/videos/formative-assessment-example-ela-sbac.

Wagner, T. (2010). *The global achievement gap: Why even our best schools don't teach the new survival skills our children need—and what we can do about it.* New York: Basic Books.

Walsh, J. A., & Sattes, B. D. (2005). *Quality questioning: Research-based practice to engage every learner.* Thousand Oaks, CA: Corwin.

Walsh, J. A., & Sattes, B. D. (2011). *Thinking through quality questioning: Deepening student engagement.* Thousand Oaks, CA: Corwin.

Wells, G. (1993). Reevaluating the IRF sequence: A proposal for the articulation of theories of activity and discourse for the analysis of teaching and learning in the classroom. *Linguistics and Education, 5,* 1–37.

Wiliam, D. (2011). *Embedded formative assessment.* Bloomington, IN: Solution Tree.

INDEX

The letter *f* following a page number denotes a figure.

ABOUT THE AUTHORS

 **Jackie Acree Walsh** is an independent educational consultant who partners with educators across the country to enhance teaching and leading in classrooms, schools, and districts. Based in Montgomery, Alabama, Jackie is also the lead consultant for the Alabama Best Practices Center, which affords her the opportunity to work with networks of school teams, district teams, instructional partners, and superintendents.

Jackie's early experience as a high school social studies teacher contributed to her passion for questioning. As a designer and facilitator of professional learning for teachers, instructional coaches, and administrators, she links quality questioning practices not only to student thinking and learning but also to adult learning and reflection. Her commitment is to collaborative design that customizes learning to the context of the learner. Her experience spans work in K–12, higher education, a regional research laboratory, and a state department of education.

The author and coauthor of numerous books and articles focused on quality questioning, Jackie seeks to make research and best practice accessible to practitioners. She received her A.B. from Duke University, M.A.T. from the University of North Carolina at Chapel Hill, and Ph.D. from the University of Alabama. Jackie can be reached at walshja@aol.com. Follow her on Twitter @Question2Think.

Beth Dankert Sattes consults through her business, Enthused Learning, primarily in the area of effective questioning in K–12 classrooms. She works with clients and staff of service centers, districts, schools, and departments of education throughout the eastern and southern part of the United States, frequently facilitating adult learning and returning (in person or via the Internet) for follow-up. Beth began her work in education as an elementary special education teacher and then as a parent educator of preschool children with behavior disorders. She holds a bachelor's degree from Vanderbilt University and a master's in early childhood special education from Peabody College. Her true love is to work with adult learners, be they teachers, administrators, instructional coaches, or parents. Her primary goal has always been to translate research-based practice into understandable and usable practice in an engaging and motivating way. She sometimes directly facilitates adult learning and sometimes trains teacher-leaders to facilitate the learning of colleagues.

With Jackie Walsh, Beth has coauthored five books, including *Thinking Through Quality Questioning, Leading Through Quality Questioning,* and *Quality Questioning.* Beth can be reached at beth@enthusedlearning.com.

Related ASCD Resources

At the time of publication, the following ASCD resources were available (ASCD stock numbers appear in parentheses). For up-to-date information about ASCD resources, go to www.ascd.org. You can search the complete archives of *Educational Leadership* at http://www.ascd.org/el.

ASCD Edge®

Exchange ideas and connect with other educators on the social networking site ASCD Edge at http://ascdedge.ascd.org/

Print Products

Better Learning Through Structured Teaching: A Framework for the Gradual Release of Responsibility, 2nd Edition by Douglas Fisher and Nancy Frey (#113006)

Content-Area Conversations: How to Plan Discussion-Based Lessons for Diverse Language Learners by Douglas Fisher, Nancy Frey, and Carol Rothenberg (#108035)

Enhancing Professional Practice: A Framework for Teaching, 2nd Edition by Charlotte Danielson (#106034)

Essential Questions: Opening Doors to Student Understanding by Jay McTighe and Grant Wiggins (#109004)

How to Design Questions and Tasks to Assess Student Thinking by Susan M. Brookhart (#114014)

Student-Led Discussions: How do I promote rich conversations about books, videos, and other media? (ASCD Arias) by Sandi Novak (#SF114069)

THE WHOLE CHILD The Whole Child Initiative helps schools and communities create learning environments that allow students to be healthy, safe, engaged, supported, and challenged. To learn more about other books and resources that relate to the whole child, visit www.wholechildeducation.org.

For more information: send e-mail to member@ascd.org; call 1-800-933-2723 or 703-578-9600, press 2; send a fax to 703-575-5400; or write to Information Services, ASCD, 1703 N. Beauregard St., Alexandria, VA 22311-1714 USA.